10 SACRED
Questions
FOR EVERY MOTHER

Stories of Joy, Pain, and Mind-blowing Love

To my
cuz Michelle.

JULIE GOHMAN, PH.D.

Love,
Julie

Clearwater Publishing House

For information please visit www.juliegohman.com

Book and Cover design by Derek Murphy.

ISBN-13: 978-0692701782

ISBN-10: 0692701788

First Edition: April 2016

10 9 8 7 6 5 4 3 2 1

To my husband Bret

with gratitude and love

Contents

Introduction

The word sacred can mean many things…

The word *sacred* refers to something of great value and importance. Something worthy of reverence. Something holy. We find what is sacred by looking at the most precious and beautiful aspects of our life. We know the sacred by what we cherish, what we protect, and what fills our heart with joy and wonder. When we encounter the light in a child's eyes, a majestic oak tree, or an exquisite piece of art, we, for just a brief moment in time, enter into the mystery that transcends ordinary existence.

Sacred, in this book, is used to describe the important process of seeking wisdom through the practice of self-inquiry. There is a desire to listen to your heart, your soul, to the still small voice that comes from within. You move beyond the surface of your life into something deeper and more meaningful. The focus is not on the answers, but on the gentle process of self-reflection and contemplation in a state of complete openness and receptivity. If you dedicate time and space to this process, you will discover what's sacred to you.

The questions I offer in this book were born from my doctoral research about motherhood. Personally, motherhood has been the most transformational experience of my life. So much about being a mother has asked me to rise up and become the greatest version of myself—to live more mindfully, give graciously, and cultivate authenticity and honesty. It's a humbling journey. Professionally, my academic background began in the field of family life and child development. I have long been interested in understanding the way our most intimate relationships, like that between mother and child, affect who we are and how we see the world.

Self-inquiry is a way for you to engage with your own story—with what is alive and active in your life right now. The questions are here for your growth, healing, and wholeness. As you quiet your mind and think about your own journey, as a child and now as a parent, you may touch sensitive and vulnerable places inside you. Self-reflection is an essential part of becoming a more conscious person. It takes courage. Silence and stillness helps. As you look within and learn to listen to your heart, understand there are no right answers. There is power in contemplating questions—even if you never come to any grand conclusions—because it opens the door to greater consciousness about life.

The women I interviewed for my study were phenomenal. It was an honor to hear their stories about motherhood. We laughed together. We cried together. We drank tea and ate lunch together. We commiserated about the challenges we face as mothers, and sighed about the overwhelming love we have for our children. In the end, I could not be more grateful for their willingness to open their hearts and share their experiences with me.

Motherhood is a sacred calling, it is a powerful part of who we are as women, and deserves more respect than it is given in our modern world. It is my wish that through these stories we may bear witness to the beautiful and enduring love of mothers everywhere.

Most of all, dear friend, I hope these stories uplift you, inspire you, and give you strength to carry on. Wherever you are on your own crazy, wonderful journey of motherhood, know that you are not alone.

In love and light,
Julie

The 10 Sacred Questions

The First Sacred Question
How can I build strong connections with my children?

The Second Sacred Question
Who am I now?

The Third Sacred Question
What do I need to be a happy mama?

The Fourth Sacred Question
What kind of Mother do I want to be?

The Fifth Sacred Question
Am I ready to let go?

The Sixth Sacred Question
What is most important to me?

The Seventh Sacred Question
Where is my circle of support?

The Eighth Sacred Question
How can I keep my marriage from falling apart?

The Ninth Sacred Question
Is there a wounded child inside me?

The Tenth Sacred Question
Am I willing to be more open, honest and vulnerable?

Morgan's Story

I love that I am connected to my kids.
We are plugged in.
—Morgan

M organ first became a mother when she was 27 years old. She had a tough labor and remembers thinking, "This is not what I thought I signed up for." When the labor was over, however, and her son was born, Morgan marveled at "God's miracle in your life that you just can't really put words to. It is almost magical in many ways. They lay those babies in your arms and it is like everything is gone from before that. You look in their little eyes and you are all they have in that moment. There are so many emotions you feel inside. I know I cried, and was smiling. You just think they are the cutest things ever. They are the most beautiful."

I just honestly was taken aback
by that strong feeling of intense love.
I was everything to my baby in that moment.

Morgan was surprised when her son was born. "You have expectations of what your babies will be, and he was not like that from the moment he was born. You kind of have presumptions what your baby will look like, and Jonah was not what I thought he was going to be. I pictured him with dark hair. I was married to a Greek at the time and he came out with reddish hair and was pale, or real fair; he looked like an angry old man. What an incredible moment."

Perhaps the biggest shock for Morgan was how much love she felt for him. "You don't think you can love someone that much. I never thought I could love someone that much. I just honestly was taken aback by that strong feeling of intense love for that baby and that I was everything to my baby in that moment. She described the feeling of love she experienced for her child as "beyond anything. You cannot explain it to anybody really."

Morgan was more nervous than she thought she would be as a new mother. "I am the youngest of ten, and so I grew up around babies all the time. I thought this would be a piece of cake; this motherhood thing will be easy. And it did, as far as loving him and being with him, but you become so cautious. I did anyway. I became so cautious that I think Jonah felt that, and so he became kind of a colicky, fussy baby. I think I worked too hard instead of just letting my natural instincts kick in. I was not in a good relationship at the time. My ex-husband was not a very healthy person. I think that translated into my emotions with Jonah, and he could feel that I am sure."

I lost me for many years.

Being a mother became all-consuming for Morgan and for many years her needs always came second. "I lost *me* for many years. It didn't help being in the relationship that I was in. I lost the importance of taking care of me through that whole process. I gave so much to my husband and my children that it took me many years to look back and find that taking care of me would make me a better mom. They always say 'take care of yourself,' but if I look back I don't know, I had no family around. It really was just my children and my husband at the time. And in the situation I was in, that was difficult to do with him not being willing to help with the children. It was just one of those things that you set aside for the time and you get rewards from your children." Morgan found fulfillment in being a mother and made it her priority to shield her children from the bad things that were happening in her marriage.

The older Morgan got, the more she became in tune with mortality. "I had a lot of worry and was consumed with worry about my children." Morgan's father was also a worrier; she remembers watching him pace the floor when she was growing up. Her children's health issues have given her many opportunities to learn how to deal with her worry.

"Jonah had some severe things; he had to have artery grafts. He was missing main arteries to his legs, and some other kinds of stuff. The doctors said, 'I think we're going to lose his leg,' when he was in surgery. Those are all such cold hard slaps in the face. I tried to do it on my own which is so goofy. I didn't want to burden anybody. It was late at night when I got that call, and my husband was sleeping with our little guy and I didn't want to wake him up. So I just sat in my own hell until I finally called my sister who lives nine hours away."

We are going to figure out how to make this better.

Her daughter has dealt with some depression, which she has made it through. Morgan credits many of the wonderful people in their life for helping them get through these health challenges and has learned "not to bury my head in the sand because it manifests itself so much bigger when you don't confront it." Her mantra is, "We are going to figure out how to make this better and if we can't make it better we are going to figure out how to work with it somehow."

Morgan's youngest son, from her second marriage, has cystic fibrosis. "He was diagnosed at 9 months, and that rocked our world for a long time." It was a time filled with anxiety for Morgan. "People couldn't tell I was a wreck, but internally, emotionally, you don't eat, you don't sleep, you are just not in a good place. I labeled Mathew for a long time in my head 'the CF child.' I went to a homeopathic person who helped treat him for a while and she said we don't want him to be the kid with CF. We are going to have him be Mathew. And you are going to be his mom. You are going to be Morgan. So, over the years, I have had to learn to let that go, quit labeling him, and let Mathew be Mathew. Let him succeed in life."

Everybody has their stuff.
Everybody has suffering in life.

A huge breakthrough for Morgan came for her one day driving down the road with her sister. "We were driving down the road and there was a woman pushing her daughter in one of those laid-back wheelchairs. I turned to my sister and I said, 'Oh, God works in funny ways.' She said, 'What?' I said, 'Mathew can feed himself, run, play, go to school, hug me. I can hug him. That mother's daughter can never do any of that.' There is always a situation where you have to look at your blessings. I can picture that moment; it was a huge moment for me, and not just about Mathew, but just looking at the situations of everybody around me. Everybody has their stuff. Everybody has suffering in life. It may come in different forms and different ways. This is where we are at, and we are going to have to dig deep, and so we did. We dug in and have made it a very positive experience. We've met wonderful people. We've gotten very involved."

I always stop now and ask myself,
'What am I to learn from this?'

"Over time I would say my biggest development through my children is spiritual. I have had to really work on trusting the Lord that where my children are and where I am is where we need to be. I have a wonderful neighbor from our cabin that told me, 'I always said to myself, what can I learn from this? What am I to learn from this?' And I think over the years and through everything I've been through I always stop now and ask myself, 'What am I to learn from this?' whether it is intellectually, spiritually, emotionally, psychologically. What is God speaking to me about right now? Take it in. It can be as simple like when Mathew wet the bed all the time. Is this something I can learn through him, or is there something he and I can learn from this? And that is really been a growth in me, taking a step back and not reacting so quickly. Just taking a moment to think these are God's children I have been given. How can I help them grow and realize maybe why they are going through what they are going through? Maybe we won't ever know, but what can we take from that and then grow in whatever area they feel it is touching them the most."

Everybody has a story,
it's what you do with that story
that forms who you are going to be.

Morgan believes that, "everybody is on a journey in life and you can either learn to take that journey and it can help you grow in areas, or you can turn your head to it and stay where you are." This attitude has allowed her to deal with the challenges she has encountered with her children with calmness and strength. "I feel like I have truly taken my experiences as a mother, wife, and used them to make me a better person. Everybody has a story, it's what you do with that story that forms who you are going to be."

Morgan describes herself as a hands-on mom. "When I grew up, my mom didn't communicate very much, well there was no sharing of feelings. So I decided early on that I was going to make sure of that. I wanted to give my children more. I wanted them to have a bigger start, and so I communicate a lot with my kids. I share with them." She reminds her children, "I am not going to be your friend, but I am here to guide you through life, and God gave you to me so I am going to give you what I know, and hopefully it will help you learn from your experiences." As a result, her children are very open with Morgan and they talk about everything together. "I love having open communication with my kids and being honest and being real. They will come to me for advice which makes me feel good as a mother that they feel comfortable to come to me and that I have done that part of my life really well, and that is rewarding."

I love having open communication with my kids
and being honest and being real.

Morgan used to be more task-oriented like her mother. "She worked hard. Her and my dad made a good partnership on a farm." Her mom always kept a very neat and clean house. "That is one thing I have worked on over the years is to just let it be, it'll still be there. If people come to my house and there are dishes in the sink, there are dishes in the sink." Morgan learned that sometimes she needs to put things aside in order to take care of her own needs. "That was a part of my mother that I have had to learn to let go." However, her mom gave her an example of spirituality that is special to Morgan. "Her faith and trust is really incredible to watch. The words that she always shared when something wasn't going right were never 'you can do this,' it was always *'we can do this. The lord didn't give this to you for no reason, we can do this.'* In our life we turn to our faith, and our church, and our leaders, and to Jesus." Morgan continues to deepen her spiritual life, and tries to teach that within her own family as well.

One of the issues Morgan has dealt with as a mother is helping her two older children navigate their relationship with their father. "My older two don't see their dad. They have seen him like twice in 14 years. We have had to have some real conversations about that, and they are real open with sharing how they feel. I have taught them a lot about 'don't carry anger in your life, it keeps you a prisoner.' It is not about the other person; really you have imprisoned yourself. I think the life lessons that I have learned I really try to share with my kids. I try not to be that helicopter parent because I know they have to go learn and yet I try to guide them while they are learning."

> *You don't want to become a prisoner*
> *within yourself where you are so angry.*

Morgan has tried to help her son and daughter learn how to set healthy boundaries, let go of the anger and resentment they have towards their father, and make good decisions for their future. "I didn't want her to be that girl that searches out for men in her life because her dad wasn't there." Morgan advised her son, "You don't want to become a prisoner within yourself where you are so angry. Your dad has no idea that you are mad at him, he's oblivious, so what good is it doing anybody?" Morgan continues to encourage her children to, "look within themselves as to what would be best for them." She keeps the lines of communication open and has been proud of the good choices her children have made.

In her first marriage, Morgan was a stepmother to her husband's daughter, who was only two at the time, and wanted her parents back together. "She was a very funny little girl." Morgan was able to be compassionate to her stepdaughter. "I had to learn to put myself in her place, to put myself in that little girl's body and mind, and what would I want? It wasn't that she didn't like me or love me; it had nothing to do with that. It was simply her own needs and wants in that moment." Morgan and her family continue to be a stable presence in her stepdaughter's life. "She loves our family. Amanda is very needy, has always been needy because of some issues with her and her dad. I have worked really hard over the years to help her realize that you can't let one person define who you are. So we are trying to help her realize that. Being a stepmother was a challenge."

I love that I am connected to my kids.
We are plugged in.

When Morgan reflected on what she most enjoys about being a mother, she said, "Oh, I love my kids. Somebody once said to me, 'If there was anything you could do,' because he was trying to figure out what I enjoy, 'what would you do?' And I said, 'I would sit on the beach with my kids.' My favorite thing is to go on family vacations with all three of them. I just love spending time with them. I love when they are all home now. I love visiting with them. I love taking them out to lunch and chatting. I love teaching them spirituality, how they can find it within themselves and how it can help them in situations." She added, "I am a proud mom. I love how my kids are developing into such good kids. I love that I am connected to my kids. We are plugged in. I am even connected to my older two with their boyfriends and girlfriends. They just sit and visit with me about stuff. I am honest, but I will tell them how it is too."

Asked what has helped the most in motherhood, Morgan said, "I think the challenges have contributed to the positiveness. Also, the people that I surround myself with. I have wonderful friends, the women in my life. And my sisters, I have been blessed to have them. Being able to vocalize and talk to other great moms and share has really been a blessing. It is definitely the women in my life, the other moms." "I have such wonderful friends that fill me up in so many ways. I am right where I need to be."

1

The First Sacred Question

How can I build strong connections with my children?

Take a moment and consider the various ways that we show love and stay connected—through our kind and uplifting words, acts of service, physical touch, gifts, and quality time spent together (*Based on Gary Chapman's 5 Love Languages*). Contemplate how you are building strong and loving connections with your children. Hint: You may want to ask your children, if they are old enough, what fills their emotional love tank. What makes them feel loved?

They, like all of us, will have a favorite love language. When you learn how to give your children what they need most to feel loved, your relationships will thrive.

- Words
- Acts of Service
- Physical Touch
- Gifts
- Quality Time

For example:

> **Words:** *I tell my children "I love you" every day. I let them know I think they are wonderful human beings, and how proud I am of who they are. I use positive messages that affirm my children's worth. I know words are powerful.*

> **Acts of Service:** *I do piles of laundry to make sure my children have clean clothes. I make their favorite foods. I sew buttons on shirts and fix bicycles. When they ask me to do something, I am happy to help.*

> **Physical Touch:** *We snuggle before bed and read stories together. Every morning I kiss their soft cheeks and say good morning. I give tender hugs and high-fives. I rub my son's back when he isn't feeling well.*

> **Gifts:** *I treat my children to pizza on Friday nights. I pick up "heart" rocks on the beach for my daughter. I buy them new clothes, shoes, and art supplies. I pick out special gifts that I think my children will truly appreciate.*

> **Quality Time:** *I look my child in the eyes and give him my full attention when he is talking to me. We play games and go for bike rides. We have real conversations. I enjoy having special time alone with each of my children.*

How can I build strong connections with my children?

Leah's Story

There is this moment where you're not a mother,
and then you are a mother.
I felt like whoa,
Who am I?
What am I?
—Leah

L eah became a mother at the age of 29. "I was really eager to get pregnant and then eager to get done with my nine months because I am a rusher. I'm a doer, so let's hurry up and get on to the next thing. The morning that she was born I woke up and when I sat up my water broke." Leah had done research, attended classes about pregnancy and birthing, and created a birth plan. "This was one of the first times in my life that I had not created this super-controlling plan about how this was all going to go down. I had never done it before and with all of the research that I had done ahead of time, I just could not get a feel for like what level of pain this was going to be. You read about many different scenarios that women have throughout their births, so I knew anything could happen."

With pregnancy, Leah's focus on controlling her body through exercise and nutrition underwent a transformation. "When I got pregnant all of that went by the wayside because I had a more important job to do. This just wasn't about me. As I went through my pregnancy, I was along for the ride and was sort of this observer as my body changed and did all this crazy stuff." She became fascinated with how, as she said, "My body has started this thing that has been happening for millions of years. I just need to sit back and listen to what my body tells me to do."

My body did this crazy thing
and out she came.

Leah's birth process was a positive and uncomplicated experience that went relatively fast after her water broke. Her contractions progressed with the aid of Pitocin (a drug to induce labor), but otherwise she took no other medications. "I was just so in the moment, doing what it was that my body was telling me to do that it never even occurred to me to step outside of that and say, I think I need help from drugs." A midwife was in attendance for her daughter's birth, but Leah did not require much assistance from her. "My body did this crazy thing and out she came. It was this baby with big eyes, blinking and looking around. I held her and the first thing I said to her was, 'Hi Ellie, I am so excited to meet you.' I had waited so long, and I knew it was going to be a girl. I immediately started breastfeeding her. She latched on great. That was the first time in my life where I gave over control and just went along with what was naturally supposed to happen. It was such an easy, beautiful, low-stress kind of thing."

What my body just did,
those are super powers.

Reflecting on her daughter's birth, Leah remembers feeling amazed at what her body could do. "Wow, what I just did right there made me totally feel super-human,

17

and there is nothing that I can't do. That, for me, lasted months and months and months and months. I am frickin' superman, what my body just did, those are super powers. Super-powers! That was huge." Even just thinking about her experience, 13 years later, Leah said she could feel the endorphins surging in her body. She was also impressed by how her body began manufacturing milk to feed her baby. "You don't have to tell it to do that. Based on how much Ellie was eating, my body would produce to match that, that was sort of crazy. I could feel my metabolism going crazy making all that milk. All she did was eat, eat, eat. She was a fat, chunky baby. She would eat a ton and spit up a ton." Through the experience of becoming a mother, Leah said that she discovered, "the power of a woman's body, up to pregnancy, during childbirth, even after."

While they were in the hospital, Leah felt like time had stopped. "We were inside yet outside of the world, like nothing else existed but this thing." As she and her husband left the hospital with their new baby on a warm day in May, she remembers observing how "everything is just so green, and bright, and beautiful." Compared to how brown it was outside when they went into the hospital, the natural world had suddenly come alive. "I also remember walking out of the hospital with that little carrier with that creepy feeling in your back like, somebody is going to stop me, they are not going to let me walk out of this hospital with this baby because I have no idea of what I am doing. In some sense I was feeling so under-prepared even though I had done all this research, because she is unique; we are unique."

We need to figure it out;
this is our journey,
And we are going to figure it out for ourselves.

When Leah settled into the rhythms of caring for a newborn, her quiet baby at the hospital turned into a colicky baby at home who cried a lot and nursed for an hour and a half at a time. A source of stress for Leah was the differences between what all the baby books recommended, what they "should" be doing (naps, feeding schedules) and what her daughter seemed to need. Her baby did not fit the "mold" of how it was supposed to go. "At a certain point, I just started ignoring all the parenting advice and realized no other mother-daughter combination has ever existed like this and will never exist again. What works for other people works for them but it might not work for us. We need to figure it out; this is our journey, and we are going to figure it out for ourselves." Her independent and determined nature helped her find her own way as a mother. Gradually over her daughter's first year of life Leah realized, "Sometimes you have to work really hard for a short period of time to lay the groundwork for something that is going to be a lot easier later on."

As a mother, Leah describes herself as consistent, very loving, and having a sense of humor. "It is just a job that I take so seriously." Leah has been nicknamed "the hammer" in her family because she is fairly strict. She takes after her mother, who is affectionately called, "the sledgehammer." Leah's mom, the epitome of strength and a source of support for Leah, was a single mom who ran a tight household when her children were growing up. "I always appreciated that but I couldn't really appreciate it until I had my own child, and then to realize that she did all of that with two, on her own, with no money. I had the happiest childhood. I had no idea that we were poor little church mice. She did such an amazing job."

However, now as a mother to her own child, there were a few things that Leah decided to do differently. "I would hope that I've created and fostered (actually all of us as her caregivers) a sense of openness in our communication. I feel like Ellie and I talk about things that my mom and I never talked about. Even an openness, like we are the total open door bathroom, walk around naked, kind of family, too. I really hope that the work we have done to lay a foundation to have those moments where you don't freak out and you don't get mad. You just calmly ask questions and have a conversation." When Leah recently asked her daughter what makes a good mom, her daughter said, "'Well, you are healthy,' and then she said, 'And you really love me.'"

> *I knew...if I stayed in a marriage*
> *that I wasn't really happy in*
> *I was not going to be*
> *the best version of myself.*

One of the biggest challenges for Leah as a mother was going through the divorce with her ex-husband. "There was good period of time right after that happened that I was convinced that I had completely ruined her life. She has no chance because I just fucked it up. That was really hard and I carried that guilt around with me for a good long time. I knew rationally that if I stayed in a marriage that I wasn't really happy in I was not going to be the best version of myself." It was a crazy and chaotic time in her life from which she learned many lessons, one being, "If you don't have a strong relationship with your partner and that relationship fails, that is going to have a huge impact on your child." Even through the stress and drama of the divorce, Leah acknowledged, "My ex-husband is a fantastic guy, and both of us recognized that the most important thing was to put Ellie's needs and priorities above our own during that process." Despite the fact that it was a hard time for all of them, their daughter is a well-adjusted kid who barely remembers the divorce. Leah is now happily married again, this time to a woman.

Leah's commitment to good communication with her daughter means they talk about everything, including spirituality and religion. "We are going to encourage her as she is growing up that if she has questions about religion we will provide those resources. If there are things she wants to explore we will gladly support that. The spiritual piece kind of comes down to exploring within yourself." Leah and her wife are mindful of teaching their values and beliefs to Ellie. "If you are not going to take part in an organized religion which gives you a set of rules as to how to live your life, then what are the rules we want to create about how we live our lives? How are we going to guide her to live her life until she is at the age where she can make those decisions for herself?"

Leah has observed that being a mother has changed her in positive ways. "Having a child helps to keep me a little more present-moment focused. As difficult as it can be to raise a child, I've also never laughed more in my life. Just seeing things through a child's eyes is so valuable as an adult. It just brings you more into that present moment and slows you down. I really appreciate what that has brought to my life as a human in general. I was a little bit surprised at how much I really, really love being a mom and how the moment she was born she became the number one priority."

If I can just shut up and listen to my body,
it will tell me exactly what it needs.

One of the most important changes for Leah as a result of pregnancy and childbirth was in her relationship to her body. "The issues that I had before I was pregnant around food and exercise and then giving up control of all of that stuff while I was pregnant made me realize afterwards that I was under a complete illusion that I ever had 100% control over my body. What I took away from that was a new ability to just listen to what my body was telling me to do. If I can just shut up and listen to my body it will tell me exactly what it needs."

By listening to her body, Leah's body became leaner and stronger after giving birth. "Once I actually stopped trying to control my body and just listened to what it told me to do, I actually then had the body that I had always worked so hard to try and get. I realized that if I would have just taken off all that pressure and force it was there all along."

"I had much more of an acceptance of my body whereas in the past it was always, this is wrong, that is wrong, got to change this, boy do I hate that. Now I just appreciate what is there. That changes everything from your physical energy, to how you sleep, to your happiness, to how you feel about your body. It is a huge shift. And as your body continues to change, as you get older, it is a whole new thing over and over again. You never have it figured out."

Who am I now?
How has being a mother changed me?

Leah's social life also changed when she became a mother. "I didn't realize before having a child that a lot of your social network becomes who your child's friend's parents are." She has a circle of friends, the mothers of her daughter's friends, whom she hangs out with on a regular basis. "I feel fortunate to have these women in my life as humans, but also as mothers. Our daughters are the same age, go to the same school, and are going through a lot of the same things together." As their children get older, Leah is conscious of new challenges in mothering. "The teenage years are the next evolution of being 2 and 3 years old, as they are gaining their independence. It is their job to test the boundaries again. I realized 'oh shit, I thought I was done with that.' This is round 2." Leah has observed significant changes in her friends as their children enter new stages of development. "Now, as women in our early 40's, our kids are becoming more independent and need us less. I feel like within my group of friends, a lot of them are changing jobs, and asking, 'do I want to stay married?' Now there is more time to focus on themselves again." Leah said they finally have, "the luxury to reflect on: Who am I now? How has being a mother changed me? How has being a wife changed me? How has my job changed me?"

I feel like my job, and my career,
actually makes me a better mom,
a better spouse, a better everything.

Leah has worked hard to strike a balance between motherhood, her other significant relationships, and her career. She is very conscious of how she spends her time and energy, knowing that it is important to find a balance for her own well-being and happiness. "At a certain point I realized that I am a much happier and fulfilled person when I am doing what I love in my work, and I am fortunate to do what I love. So I feel like my job, and my career, actually makes me a better mom, a better spouse, a better everything. As an entrepreneur I like that I am setting a different example for her that I never ever saw when I was growing up. I have a huge sense of responsibility for giving her everything that she needs, not from a 'things' perspective, but love and reliability and consistency and all that kind of stuff."

What does a mom look like?
What does a mom do?

Reflecting on her early days as a mother, Leah realized she went through an identity crisis. "After Ellie was born I went through this bizarre shit in my identity because all of a sudden I have this title of 'Mother.' What does a mom look like? I started dressing weirdly, conservatively. What does a mom do? I was not comfortable in my own skin. And being a mother also changes your sexual identity. I think it took me about a year to realize that I can still be the exact same person that I was before she was born. I can still be a mother who dresses funky. At one time I felt like I had to play the role of mother, dowdy mother. It was an additional title that came on. There is this moment where you are not a mother, and then you are a mother. I felt like whoa, who am I? What am I? I realized the whole thing was actually an evolution that took a long time. I was still me throughout that whole entire process. I am still me now. I don't have to give up who I am to be a mom."

"I wonder for anybody if it really turns out to be like they think, or thought, it was going to. Sometimes from the perspective before having children, I don't think you even have the capacity to even speculate about the experiences that you are going to have as a parent, or how it is going to change you." Motherhood continues to be a joy and a challenge that Leah meets with great enthusiasm and dedication. She describes it this way, "As for being a mom—I'm all in!"

The Second Sacred Question

Who am I now?

Consider how motherhood has affected who you are:

- Socially
- Emotionally
- Mentally
- Creatively
- Spiritually
- Physically

Contemplate the following questions:

- Do you have nourishing relationships in your life?
- What emotional issues are you dealing with?
- How do you express yourself creatively?
- What are your dreams and plans for the future?
- Did your spiritual or religious beliefs change when you became a mother?
- How do you feel about your body?

Who am I now?

Rose's Story

God is in the water,
and the little otter swimming across,
and certainly in the babies and the children.
—Rose

R ose became a mother for the first time when she was 20 years old; however, the feeling of being a mother was nothing new to her. "I was a little mother most all of my life. I was changing diapers when I was 8 and babysitting for neighbors when I was 9 and 10." She was the oldest of seven kids growing up and helped care for many babies. "It wasn't strange to have a baby and I knew how to do things. I think it is hard for young women who are just dropped into that, who don't have any experiences, who haven't babysat or who haven't had younger children around, nieces or nephews."

Still, having her baby was an exhilarating experience. "I was so excited that I couldn't sleep. In those days they didn't let you keep the baby so I had just a couple of minutes and then they took him away." Rose had a long hard delivery. "They put Jacob in an isolette because the labor had been so long. They said he had too much guck in his lungs, and so I didn't get to hold him for a couple of days. It was horrible." Rose shared a room in the hospital with a young lady who wasn't keeping her baby. "She was really sad. The first hours of my motherhood I listened to somebody's really sad story.

Neither one of us went to sleep." Eventually another new mother came in, and Rose was finally able to hold her new baby boy. "The next woman was a minister's wife. She was kind of naughty, and shocking, and daring. She was just a charming companion and we had a great time with those two babies."

Rose's life changed dramatically after she went home from the hospital with her first son. Her husband was working and then went back to school a few months after their baby was born. "The days were really long. Pregnant mothers in my circle did not work, and new mothers of newborns didn't work, so I was alone all day long. It was like night and day difference for me, going to school and working and living in a busy household, to then being all alone with a new baby all day and all night." Rose eventually had two more sons and then became pregnant with her fourth child.

"My fourth one, I didn't get to see him or hold him until he was 6 days old. That was horrible. They took him, my fourth son, because he had a disease. The technology that saved him had not previously been available so we were really lucky. They took him by ambulance immediately after he was born by C-section. So I never got to see him." The hospital staff whisked him away and sent Rose back to her room. "My mom and dad and Joe (her husband) had seen the baby. I had been on a cart and they could have wheeled me down to see the baby but they didn't, they brought me back to my room and moved me back to the bed. All these years later, it still makes me mad. Joe didn't know how to fight for me, and my parents didn't know how to fight for me. They just accepted the rules."

Their baby boy had to spend his first days and weeks in a special unit where he was treated for his disease. "When

I finally did see him, he was just this cuddly little ball. He still had a lot of hair on his body and he was real blonde and fuzzy and sweet. We couldn't hold him. We had to put our hands inside the isolette and cradle him with our hands." Rose's husband was working in Chicago at the time and had to go back while their baby was still in the hospital.

Isn't this too much for you grandpa?
And he said, Oh, no. Babies need their mamas.

Rose's grandpa stepped in to help. "He would drive out, because I couldn't drive because of the C-section, and he would pick me up and he would take my 4-year old home with him for the day, and got me to the hospital so I could spend all day with the baby. Then he would do the reverse back and pick me up. He would usually feed me dinner, and then take us all back home. It was a minimum of 2 hours in the car every day for him. I said to him, 'Isn't this too much for you grandpa?' And he said, 'Oh, no. Babies need their mamas.'"

It was a wonderful moment when they were finally able to bring their fourth baby boy home. Rose remembers how happy and full of smiles her others boys were. "All the brothers, how overjoyed they were to finally have their little brother home."

Rose spent many years at home with her children. "I really love traditional homemaking. I love to cook. I love to sew. There were a lot of things I didn't love, like the diapers, but I really enjoyed being home. I really enjoyed being with the kids. I really enjoyed having a house full of kids, and their friends, not just mine."

As her children got older Rose went back to work and established a successful career as an educator. Reflecting back on those years at home, Rose is thankful for all the time she had at home with her boys. Being a mother to boys helped her in her career many times. For example, at a national conference one year Rose was in charge of a children's program where there was a group of boys that had gotten restless by the middle of the week, and Rose knew just how to work with them. "I came back and I thanked my sons. Everybody else was overwhelmed by this boy energy, but I could really love it and embrace it, and the boys showed me such a great time. My boys taught me how to connect to boy energy."

*Our kids have always
been important to us.*

Rose and her husband raised their four sons surrounded by friends and family, and when asked what helped them the most during those years of busy childrearing, Rose had a ready answer. "I think in part the answer is community. We have had an extended family with shared values. We have had church communities with shared values. I think there is a measure of luck in there. I think we tried to do the right thing. Our kids have always been important to us."

When Rose gives parenting and marital advice to parents of young children she encourages them to find time alone together. "Having some alone time without interruptions is really important for parents. If we didn't have time to go for dinner, we would get up early and go Saturday morning and get back before the kids were up (when they were teenagers). Just do the right thing, and then hope for the best."

A great source of joy for Rose throughout motherhood has been her path of feminine (women's) spirituality. Some years ago she was asked to write a piece about what women's spirituality means to her. "My answer was that my core spirituality is being on a boat on a lake and watching the otters swim by, or holding a new baby, or when my little grandson came over about two weeks before Christmas and came in the back door and said, 'I'm here grandma, I'm here, I'm here, I'm here.' Those are the peak spiritual experiences for me. It's not about being in a church or about having a decades-old ritual; it is about moments of intense feeling with nature or with children, or with my husband. It's so interwoven it is hard to talk about or separate it out."

Rose belongs to a spiritual community comprised of women. "It is very much earth-based spirituality, but silly and playful at the same time." Rose has spent a lot of time delving into feminine forms of spirituality. Her ideas about God have naturally evolved. "When I began to look and see that god was first primarily female across cultures, it opened everything up. I discarded the idea that there is only one right way. So God is in the water, and the little otter swimming across, and certainly in the babies and the children."

That is a major shift,
to be responsible for a life,
24 hours a day, 7 days a week.

Rose has been committed for decades to both feminism and motherhood. She has noticed several trends in our society. "I think there is an aggrandizement of young teenage women, and women into their early adulthood." Yet she maintains that some things remain the same for women. "I think there are some major shifts when they get married. They are still expected to do a lot of the grunt work in a relationship and household. I still think for many women the major shift is when they become mothers, even though it is different from the 1950's and 1960's when I came of age. That is a major shift, to be responsible for a life, 24 hours a day, 7 days a week, whether you are actually the one doing it or not, to be responsible. That still falls disproportionately on women."

Rose believes that motherhood is a key issue that feminists need to keep talking about, especially the economic impact upon women when they become mothers. "When Joe and I got married, we said 'we are a team and we are going to raise this family together. Joe is going to work outside the home, and Rose is going to work inside the home, and we are a team and we are equals.' Those were just our assumptions. In reality, he was getting all kinds of things that I wasn't getting."

*I was more worried
about raising boys than girls.*

As a mother to boys, Rose was concerned about the cultural influences that affected them. "When I was young and thought about having boys I was more worried about raising boys than girls. It seemed that boys were more exposed to drugs and alcohol and bigger societal problems, and that girls' problems would be more homebound. So that was a big worry. I think the messages that the culture sends boys and men are not healthy messages." For Rose the answer was finding healthy role models and creating a strong community of support for her sons. "I am so glad they had a good dad. My husband had my good dad and my good grandfathers, and my uncles. They were a community of good, caring, nurturing men." Rose's sons continue to be a strong source of support for one another. "They get along well with each other and they help each other. That gives both Joe and I great pleasure. They are all good men now and they are all such good dads. It is great to see. When challenges or hardships occur, as they have over the years, they are there for one another. I think it is really important for men to have other good men in their lives."

I have a deep love of children.
I can't imagine my life without it.

Being a mother has been core to Rose's identity, and motherhood has been a prominent part of what she has studied and taught about in her work. She remembers a follow-up survey from a workshop she conducted with mothers and fathers that asked them a question about their identity. When did you most feel like a man? And, when did you most feel like a woman? "The men said they most felt like a man when they were having intercourse, and the women said they most felt like a woman when they became a mother." For women it was giving birth and nursing. The results, although they were surprising in some ways, resonated deeply with Rose's personal feelings about motherhood. "I can't imagine not having children. I grew up nurturing children, knowing I wanted to do that. I have a deep love of children. I can't imagine my life without it."

Rose and her husband are now proud grandparents to many grandchildren. "We love being grandparents, just love it." Family continues to be important to them, and they enjoy spending time with their children and grandchildren. "We have cousin camp every year." Rose and her husband have some of the grandkids over to their house at the end of summer for a week. Rose and her grandchildren plan fun activities, looking for enriching things to do. "That is the kind of grandparents we are, they go to a lot of museums and hear a lot of music and they see art."

"The grandparent issue is that time is so much more precious. We blink our eyes and they go from being toddlers to walkers. It's just so fast. When I was a mother it felt like forever. It felt like forever I would have Cheerios on the floor and breadcrumbs and have to sweep two or three times a day. The whole time thing has changed as we age and so being with the children seems really important." Rose and her husband feel fortunate to be able to watch their grandchildren grow up. Rose jokes that they need a bumper sticker on their car that says, "This car stops at every concert, sports event, and play." They are proud of their grandchildren who are successful kids and good students. "Grandparenting is pretty much all joy."

Serena's Story

Family is a gift. Kids are a gift.
—Serena

Serena first became a mother at the age of 27 years old. "My husband and I had been trying for a good two years to get pregnant. I was working in a level two nursery at the time with other nurses who were also trying to get pregnant. We were all giving each other tips; like our husbands should wear boxer shorts and we shouldn't have heater blankets. It was fun. Actually, we all got pregnant about the same time. I think the boxer shorts helped. So we were very excited. I knew that I always wanted to be a mom." Serena remembers the moment she found out she was pregnant. "I remember incredible joy when the test was positive, and my husband was very happy too."

Serena's pregnancy went well but her birthing experience did not go as she had hoped. "It was hard and I'm not sure I had the best health care at that time either. I ended up having a C-section." She decided she didn't want to go through another C-section if she could help it. "It was a benefit working with nurses who were moms. They helped coach me through it the next time around. I interviewed everyone, and asked, 'How did you push?' Because I think I pushed ineffectively and didn't have good coaching during that time. It's quite a difference to have a vaginal birth versus a C-section. I recovered so much faster." The rest of Serena's five children were born vaginally.

I loved those days of the children being young.
We just had a certain harmony.

Settling into life with little children was a smooth transition for Serena. "I really enjoyed motherhood. I loved those days of the children being young. We just had a certain harmony. My kids didn't really fight with each other. We used time-outs as punishment, and rarely had to do that. There was just a certain calm in the house that was sweet. I really enjoyed it." Early on, Serena knew that she wanted to change the family patterns that she had grown up with. "I worked hard to create a family and a life that was different from my upbringing."

Serena talks happily about how she and her husband, who is also very patient and loving, chose to raise their family. "I had patience, and loved to read to my kids. We enjoyed lots of road trips. It was good and refreshing." Serena credits her husband as being a wonderful father to their children, and a good source of support to her. "I was glad I chose a good man in my life. That was my other family pattern, to choose very dysfunctional, typically alcoholic men, making very poor choices that way."

When I was with the kids,
I was really with them.

Serena found herself at a point in motherhood when she was not as satisfied with being a full-time mother. She felt ready for a change and a need to explore what else she wanted to do. "I think it was when the kids were older that

I realized that I had become kind of robotic. I was meeting all of their needs and doing dishes and making meals. I remember distinctly one day washing the dishes and thinking, 'there's got to be more than this.' Even though I loved it, it didn't hold as much weight for me in its entirety. So I went back to school and got a Master's degree and it was great for me. It was a really good balance to go back to school and back to work. I found I had more energy even around the house. And when I was with the kids, I was really with them, instead of the assumption that we are always together. I thought it was good for the kids to see me go back to work too. And for Dad to do some dishes, and the kids to pitch in more. It was a balancing act but it was a good one."

Being a mother for Serena has felt like a journey of discovery made possible by her children's presence. "In a lot of ways you are growing with your kids. You are revisiting athletic events and their education. In a way it features how you are becoming inquisitive with them. That was fun. We are really big into books in my family and reading. We all read books together. We all read the Narnia series together, and chapter books. We would all crawl onto the bed and read. It was fun, through their eyes, to experience those things, the world of imagination, and their excitement and passion for life. For me, it was the nurturing, enjoying that, being present to them also. It made me more tuned in, tapped in emotionally too. It was kind of a full circle thing."

I didn't realize what I had missed
until I started raising kids.

Serena realized as she was raising her children that her mother had never read to her when she was growing up. "There wasn't a lot of security in my home. My father was an alcoholic. So bedtimes were really important to me; I wanted to know my kids were tucked in and safe. I didn't realize what I had missed until I started raising kids. In a lot of ways you go back into the holes of your life when you grow up in a dysfunctional family. As you raise children you see what was good in your growing up years and you notice what you were missing."

Being a mother to five children has given Serena the opportunity to observe how unique each child is. "My life has been so enriched by each of them. They are each so different, all of them. They are each so very different in how they experience life and how they express themselves." Serena is watching her children turn into adults at this stage in motherhood. "It's neat now that they have this life of their own too. When we have family dinners it's like they fill up the space. They love being together. They value each other too. It's always amazing. It's really a gift now. All those years of the work of it, changing diapers and wiping noses, getting them to appointments, to having this next phase of life where the kids are friends to each other and call me and ask me how I am doing, or know something big is happening in our lives and ask us about that. Family is a gift. Kids are a gift."

Serena's devotion to mothering has also impacted her work as a nurse on an adolescent psychiatric unit for kids. "Most of them are suicidal, some of them have behavioral problems too, and are oppositional; some kids have done time in juvenile detention. In a way there is a big part of me that is very nurturing, and empathetic, and soft, but you also have to learn how to be tough. It's been a good job. I really like it. I love the people I work with. I really like the kids. I feel like there is a part of me that is mothering. And if kids react negative to me, sometimes it's just transference from their own mom. I'm kind of the mom on the unit. I get it."

We are very involved in their lives,
but I've also had to learn how to step back too.

As her children get older, Serena is focused on instilling a sense of personal responsibility in her children. She and her husband both put themselves through college, and now they ask their kids to work for part of their college tuition. "We are very involved in their lives, but I've also had to learn how to step back too."

Describing herself as a mother, Serena says she is "nurturing but real." "I started out being a micro-manager. It's about control, because my early life was out of control, so I try to control a lot of things. I realized that I have stepped back a lot. I've had to remember the humor and to take the long view on a lot of things. I have a daughter with really bad attention deficit disorder, and she is a challenge to parent. She is great, and brilliant, and funny, and she is great to talk with, but she is very disorganized, whereas I am very organized. So I bite my tongue a lot and let her figure it out."

Now I feel like I'm their cheerleader.

Serena's role as a mother to older children means she is always encouraging them to do their best as individuals. "My mom was absent in a lot of ways but on the side she was a cheerleader too. We found resilience in it. I think I'm that way with my kids. I'm a cheerleader with them. I'm probably more like my (maternal) grandmother. She was strong, she was faith-filled, she was always learning. She was very compassionate. She was a gifted writer. She was an amazing woman. When I came home from college I mostly went to visit her. I spent a lot of time with my grandparents. She was my rock."

Serena's oldest four children are no longer at home most of the time, so when the whole family comes together it is special. "I look forward to them coming home, playing board games. Now I feel like I'm their cheerleader. It is fun to see them doing things to cheer and look forward to. I enjoy being together at the holidays, the celebrations of life."

Like every mother, Serena has had her share of challenges. "James went through a serious depression when he was in high school. That was hard. Even though I worked in the field it is really hard to parent because they slip into patterns you want to fix and you can't. They won't get out of bed and they are suicidal. So that was a very tough time. It was tough not to be depressed with him, not to worry 24 hours a day, seven days a week. That was a particular challenge. And my 22-year-old daughter was in intensive care on life support. She had pneumonia that overwhelmed her body when she was 15. She went from being a healthy girl to being on a ventilator and having blood transfusions. That was a scary time too. Very tough."

*Friendships have always
been important to me.*

When asked what has contributed to her positive experiences in motherhood, Serena answered, "I think having good friendships, but I would have to say first it is valuing children and childbirth, that experience of valuing being a mom." Serena also cites her life experiences before she became a mother. "I worked in Mexico for four months and I traveled to Europe before I became a mom. So I did have a life outside of that. I didn't feel like I had missed things. I was really ready to be a mom when we became parents. Friendships have always been important to me. From high school on I created that, and was blessed with really good friends who are still really good friends to me today."

Serena also credits her husband as being a major source of support. "Dave is very much hands-on and we agree a lot. Neither one of us were harsh disciplinarians so we really are compatible in that way in parenting." Earlier in their lives, Serena remembers doing most of the work with the children. "The first seven years of starting a business he worked seven days a week, so I did single parenting for quite a number of years. He went through a depression too, so for a couple of years it was really hard. There were years I was a single parent in many ways. Even though he had to do that, he was still supportive."

You just see what they have inside of them;
it is amazing.

As Serena and her family have grown over the years they have been reevaluating their belief system. "I was in a spiritual quandary because we were in a fundamental group and had to break that down and deconstruct it to really figure out who God was in our lives." Serena disliked the way the group wanted parents to "mold" their children. "I had always thought it was pretty repressive, so thankfully I moved away from having that pressure in my life to make them be something." Serena has chosen to nurture the individuality of each of her children. "You just see what they have inside of them; it is amazing. Each of them is so unique in character. Yet you realize there is a bigger dimension in life, that the universe is so much bigger. There is such a spiritual dimension to life. You are co-creator, co-experiencer of it. You see people grow and become who they should be, and embrace life in their own ways."

Family life is the foundation that Serena feels is most important for her children. "I think family is one of the most powerful institutions in the world. It is what reverberates in the children, like kids who are accepting, and don't hold prejudices. They are each very loving in their own ways. I've had that personal journey with each of my kids. They are all very amazing people. We have really great talks about life and meaning. I'm not constricted to one form of relating to God. I've grown. It kind of took me going through that master's program to break down some scripts I was given. To see that homosexuality is okay, that Christianity doesn't have to be the only way, to be more diverse and accepting. To think for themselves has been big with my kids."

My kids blow me away some times.

Serena enjoys watching her children put their beliefs into action. "They have all done acts of mercy and kindness in their lives. Mark and Jill worked at an orphanage in Costa Rica. My oldest son went out of his way to go to my great nephew's band concert on a week he had finals. James spent nine months in South Africa at a daycare that provided free daycare for single working mothers in a very poor area. To me, that is the beauty of faith or spirituality—how it plays out in your character and how you treat other people. My kids blow me away some times."

The Third Sacred Question

What do I need to be a happy mama?

Reflect on the following list of qualities that happy mamas exhibit in their life (in random order).

- Having a supportive partner who is an active parent
- Caring for your self
- Finding a healthy balance between work and home
- Laughing
- Developing a strong and resilient nature
- Making a deep commitment to motherhood
- Setting boundaries
- Making changes that honor your needs and desires
- Valuing family
- Nourishing friendships with other women
- Growing and learning
- Reaching out for help when you need it

- Self-awareness
- Letting go
- Creating a calm, harmonious family environment
- Choosing to be peaceful
- Taking the long view
- Acknowledging your own childhood wounds
- Being grateful
- Honoring your children's freedom and individuality
- Being open and honest
- Living according to your values and beliefs
- Being present in the moment

**Now contemplate what you personally need to be a happy mama.

What do I need to be a happy mama?

Paulina's Story

However you are, they are going to be.
Not what you say, but how you are.
Whatever path you show them,
they are going to follow.
—Paulina

Paulina had her first child when she was 26 years old. "I almost think that when I was told I was pregnant was when I first became a mother. I started rocking his clothes and stuff like that. I was so excited." Paulina had been a nanny before going to college, and between different things had done daycare, so she felt confident about taking care of a baby. "The day he was born I was induced because I had preeclampsia. They broke my water and I had to labor about 22 1/2 hours. I was put on Pitocin. I never got past a three so I had to have a C-section." Paulina's mother had experienced numerous C-sections and subsequent bad complications, and therefore both she and Paulina were in a panic. "I was getting so worked up about having a C-section that they almost wanted to put me under completely. I was just getting so upset."

Paulina's husband was a source of quiet strength through labor and delivery. "My husband was so great the morning of, getting me a little bit of toast and juice." In the process of making toast he set off the fire alarm at the hospital. "I thought that was really sweet and endearing that he went to a different area and made toast. He was just bound and determined that I have my toast. He is such a sweet husband. When I was laboring and feeling disgusting. He was like, 'you are just so beautiful.' He is the one person in my life that has made me feel incredibly special, him and my children. I didn't get that growing up in my home. This just makes up for all that." Her husband's encouragement is important to Paulina. "There is a lot of love and tenderness. He gives me a lot of courage. I was able to go through the C-section."

That is the day I felt the most in love
with my husband,
watching him become a father.

Some of Paulina's most precious memories were in the moments right after her son's birth, watching her husband with their new baby. "Our son held his hand and he was just like, 'oh my gosh, my son held my hand.' That is the day I felt the most in love with my husband, watching him become a father." Her mother was also there to hold her new grandson. "That part was so special to me. Being there and watching my mom become a grandma. Me becoming a mom was great too. but I was reveling in watching these important people with him."

While they were in the hospital with their new baby, her husband quickly became a protective father. "My husband, security and military guy, set up an obstacle course in our room. He put all these things in the way and put the bassinet on the very side so if anybody came into our room they had to get through all these things in the way. They had to get through him, and then me." Paulina looks back fondly on her son's birth even though he became jaundiced and had to be put in the NICU under lights, a stressful event for her and her husband as new parents. "It was a great day that I became a mom." Less than 2 years later, Paulina had another baby boy, and then a daughter 5 years later.

When my husband first got deployed
I got very depressed.

Paulina's husband is in the military, which proved to be a challenge for her as a young mother. "When my husband first got deployed I got very depressed and I did seek out help. I went to a psychologist and he said, 'Well, so what if your husband dies. You still have your own life, and you still have the lives of these kids, (it was just my two boys at the time). These two boys are counting on you. Your life doesn't begin and end with your husbands.' He says, 'children are like little ducklings, however the mother will be, the children will be. They will fall right in line.' I always took that to heart and always lived by that."

Paulina became a single mother when her husband was deployed and found herself overwhelmed at times. "The work it takes to be a mother, to have all these little lives that count on you is just so tremendous." However, Paulina was proactive in finding help when her husband was absent. "Even though there is a lot of work, there is a lot of joy."

As a mother, Paulina realized she was the primary example of how to live for her children. "You are just much more accountable because your children are a reflection. However you are, they are going to be. Not what you say, but how you are. Whatever path you show them, they are going to follow. I have always taken that responsibility very seriously, to really live my ideals so that they will too."

I have to be in charge
and I have to be on my game.

Being a mother to not only one, but two children with special needs has also proven to be a challenge for Paulina (her oldest son and daughter are both on the spectrum for autism). "I have to be in charge and I have to be on my game as far as the structure, or they will be all out of sorts and not be able to manage the next day. That is the struggle, the everyday struggles, especially with kids with special needs. They are relentless. They never let up. It is a lot, especially when you are alone as a single parent. That would be my biggest hurdle as a mother, is trying to do as much as I can, and get everything done."

Whether her children have special needs or not, Paulina sees the best in each of them. "I just really love my children with everything that I have. Being able to pour that love into them and get that love back is amazing. I really love who my children are." She has enjoyed watching her children form a strong bond as siblings; they play together, help each other, and even cry for one another sometimes. Both of Paulina's sons adore their little sister. "When she was a little baby, and the boys were big into knights, they bent on their knee, and said, 'Michelle, princess Michelle, we swear our allegiance to you. We'll be your knights in shining armor.' And they have been true to their word."

A stupid woman
refuses help when it is offered,
a smart woman
takes help when it is offered,
and a wise woman
seeks out help when it is needed.

At one point in motherhood, Paulina experienced serious issues with her weight. She was having difficulty getting it under control and realized she needed to do something. "They say, 'a stupid woman refuses help when it is offered, a smart woman takes help when it is offered, and a wise woman seeks out help when it is needed.' I really needed help. I couldn't get that part under control. I was a stay-at-home mom and didn't do anything. I was always bigger to begin with, and it was something I really couldn't control after my husband's deployment, and being in the house, just me, and my kids. It was something that I had to seek out help for. I think I wouldn't have been as serious about my health if it wasn't for my children." Paulina decided to have gastric bypass surgery and lost 150 pounds. She wanted to show her kids a good example of how to be the person you wanted to be, and so she got the help she needed.

There are many ways that motherhood has inspired Paulina to strive to achieve her goals. "I feel like when you have children you are able to think outside yourself; it gives you that ability. I think that is so important for maturity. You can look beyond your years. When my children came and they started talking and I was able to communicate with them I wanted to make sure I was being the person that I wanted to be, like going back to college, finishing my degree. I lost my weight. I try to be their example." Despite coming from poverty, being overweight, and not doing well in school when she was younger, becoming a mother gave her a new motivation to succeed in life. "With my children, with them, I was always trying to push myself to be a better person. I think they have helped me grow. Without them I don't think I would have pushed myself."

*It can be so overwhelming
and so heartbreaking.*

As a mother of two special needs children, Paulina strives to do her best to help them with their challenges. "It can be so overwhelming and so heartbreaking. It is so much, so overbearing, all the research, just trying to figure everything out from diet and health to medicine." Working full time and taking care of her three children at home, often alone, has affected how she sees her job as a mother. "I try to get as much as I can accomplish done. It's like driving on ice; you just hope you are going the right way. It's okay that I'm not perfect, to allow myself to be okay with that, just be good enough. Good enough to get by is okay, good enough to be normal, because that is what I want for my son too, being a mother of a special education person. It is such a struggle to just get to that average, normal thing."

I've had to sacrifice a lot for my kids.

Paulina has sometimes felt judged by other women because of who she and her children are. "If you don't fit in this certain little box there is so much pressure. It can be overwhelming. So I say forget it, I don't care. I don't care about fitting in that box. That's okay." Paulina focuses instead on doing what is best for her children. "Socially and emotionally, I've had to sacrifice a lot for my kids." She has found herself in places and situations that have not always been easy to deal with. Through it all, Paulina continues to put her children first, and finds great joy in motherhood.

Paulina has been fortunate to have the support of many special people in her life, including her husband's mother. "She means a great deal to me. If I needed help at any time

I could call her. She would come. And she is always telling me to take care of myself. She is always trying to make sure that I have enough support emotionally. She has been great like when I was going to college and I had my finals. She took the kids during the finals week. She was responsible for them. She came and lived with us for finals week so the kids wouldn't be out of their environment and stuff like that, and she would have dinners ready for me."

Paulina has also been successful in reaching out when she knew she could not do it all herself. "When my husband was deployed I needed help managing the house, for house chores and stuff like that, so I put an ad in the paper and I hired a high school girl." Paulina and her children became very close to the high school girl they hired, and the girl's family. "They have stuck by me as a mother and supported me every time my husband is deployed." They spend a lot of time together, and have become good friends. "Now they are like an additional in-law family to me. They are people I can count on and support me emotionally." Paulina calls them the "lock-in-laws." Paulina also has a sister in California and her mother whom she talks to, but says that because of the distance she relies more on her in-laws and lock-in-laws.

The whole process
of becoming a mother
is so miraculous.

Paulina appreciates the time she has with her children. "The best part of being a mom is that I get to spend all this time with these three people who are really awesome. It's kind of like I hit the jackpot because I get to be around these really cool, awesome kids. I don't have to pay anybody to be around them. They are just mine. They are mine and I get to spend time with them at any time I want. I feel so blessed for these three people. They are so amazing."

Paulina's faith helps her focus on the good in her life and in her children instead of focusing on the difficulties. "I think being a mother really makes you live your faith. You have this miracle of God staring you in the face all the time. The whole process of becoming a mother is so miraculous."

Christian values are important to Paulina but she has also passed along some traditions that she grew up with. "There are some Native American spiritual beliefs that my dad passed on like the burning of the sage, the smudging, and some other certain aspects about feeling close to the earth that I do talk to my kids about." She is glad to find her children have received them with an open mind and heart so far.

I think that every child is good,
absolutely a gift from God.

As a mother, Paulina finds joy in watching her children. "I think that every child is good, absolutely a gift from God. They are our gift in this world from him." Their "child-like hearts" inspire Paulina. "Being closer to them and having that kind of heart helps me to be closer to God, because they are such an example of having the awe, and wonder, and gratefulness that God always wants us to have."

4

The Fourth Sacred Question

What kind of Mother do I want to be?

Consider your personal strengths and the qualities that you value. How do these qualities manifest in your everyday life as a mother?

Add and change your list until it looks like the mother you want to be!

Some Examples:

Quality	My Everyday Life
Healthy	I exercise and eat healthy foods.
Kind	I reach out and help others.
Organized	Our home is clean and orderly.
Ambitious	I set goals and work towards them.
Loyal	Trust and integrity are important to me.
Attentive	I am aware of my children's needs.
Prosperous	I make wise decisions about money.
Devoted	I put our family first.
Resilient	I have made it through difficult times.

Passionate	I am full of energy and enthusiasm.
Peaceful	I do not argue about petty things.
Open-Minded	I enjoy hearing new ideas.
Generous	Giving to others brings me joy.
Honest	I take responsibility for my actions.
Creative	I am curious and full of imagination.
Adventurous	I love traveling new places.
Optimistic	I try to focus on the good.
Mindful	It is my intention to be fully present.
Confident	I believe in myself.
Grateful	Everyday I count my blessings.
Resourceful	I can make do with very little.
Patient	I am the queen of calmness.
Strong	I know how to survive and thrive.
Funny	Laughing makes everything better.
Supportive	I encourage and help my children.
Trustworthy	You can count on me.
Artistic	I honor my creative gifts.
Loving	I am warm and affectionate.
Intelligent	Gaining knowledge is important to me.
Fair	I am objective and evenhanded.
Spiritual	I value my connection to the divine.
Humble	My ego is not in control of me.
Respectful	I am courteous and considerate.
Compassion	My heart is tender when I see suffering.
Playful	I make time to have fun with my family.
Authentic	I'm not afraid to be who I really am.
Joyful	My attitude is sunny and lighthearted.
Balanced	I am mentally and emotionally stable.

What kind of Mother do I want to be?

Jasmine's Story

Despite your best intentions and planning and learning
you just can't control what is going to happen
and who they are,
you have to roll with it.
—Jasmine

Jasmine became a mother when she was 30 years old. When she reflected on when she first felt like a mother she said, "I think it was actually the first time I was pregnant, which ended in a miscarriage. It was devastating to me." That was several years before her son was born. "We weren't planning on having a baby at that point, but then I just knew, 'I'm ready to be a mom, I want to be a mom.'" After the miscarriage, Jasmine had a tubal pregnancy. "We had started a fertility work-up to see what was going on. It is a lot of going in and blood tests and all this stuff. I don't know if I felt relieved, like okay, we're going to figure it out now, but then I got pregnant."

I knew a lot about childbirth
and I knew exactly how I wanted it to happen
…and of course it didn't happen that way.

At 6 weeks they were relieved to find a heartbeat, a good sign in her pregnancy. "I planned a home birth. I knew I

Julie Gohman, Ph.D.

always wanted to have a home birth. We found a midwife, and I also got nurse midwife care so it was like a dual track just in case I needed to go to the hospital. I didn't want to walk in without knowing anyone or having a relationship with anyone so my plan was to not show up for the birth at the hospital. I knew a lot about childbirth and I knew exactly how I wanted it to happen and worked hard to have it happen that way, and of course it didn't happen that way."

When the time came, 2 1/2 weeks after her due date, Jasmine labored at home for a long time. "My contractions, after I was pushing for a while, got really spaced out again and less intense. We had to work with that for about 8 hours. Then my midwife said I needed Pitocin." At the hospital, surrounded with her doulas and her favorite nurse midwife, she got the Pitocin, but it did not work. Even though Jasmine had wanted a girl, she suspected that it was a boy that was holing up inside her. Eventually she ended up having a C-section.

If plan A doesn't work
you have to go to plan B.

"I was just so happy, he was there and he came and he was so beautiful and big." "Of course I was sad about the way the delivery process went down but it was the best thing that could have happened to me because I just learned that if plan A doesn't work you have to go to plan B, and guess what, plan A doesn't work most of the time when you are a parent, when you are a mom." Looking back, Jasmine felt like the birthing experience pushed her right into motherhood. "This is what it's going to be like, despite your best intentions and planning and learning you just can't control what is going to happen and who they are, you have to roll with it."

Motherhood was not quite what Jasmine expected. "First of all, I have always liked kids, I always babysat, and I was older. I just thought this isn't going to be that hard. I'm going to be really good at this. I definitely had no idea what it meant to be a mom, and to be a mom of a kid that you didn't think you would ever have. I sometimes tease my son and say, "what happened to my quiet little girl that sits and colors pictures?"

I don't sugarcoat a lot of things.
I think that is a black parenting style.

She discovered when she became a mother that she is much like her father, who was the strict parent in her house growing up. "I try to be aware of that but I also knew at the end of the day that my dad loved me, and that he was doing the best that he could." Her dad considered it his job to make sure she succeeded in the world, and now Jasmine feels the same way about her son. "I don't sugarcoat a lot of things. I think that is a black parenting style. My dad is black and was raised in the south and raised in Jim Crow. In that situation you don't have chances to mess up because you could be hanging from the next tree. He always said you have to be better because you are black, and that is just the way it is. Even though Ryan, her son, doesn't look black, he has super curly hair, and you can tell he is something. He is fair, and has green eyes like his dad, and lighter brown hair. But he's black. His mom is black and his grandpa is black. I take that really seriously as a mom raising a black boy even if he doesn't look like he is."

Jasmine's identity also changed after she had her son. "I feel like before anything else I am a mom." Now that she is dating again after her recent divorce from Ryan's father, she is trying to balance being a mother with developing a new relationship with somebody else. She feels that anyone new in her life would have to know her as a mother and would have to be good to her son. "It is just who I am at my core and I don't remember what it was like not being a mom." At this point she is cautious to bring a new man into her son's life.

Being a mother has also shaped how Jasmine attends to her life. Before having her son, she found it easy to walk away from or avoid difficult or scary situations. "You can't do that as a mom even though you are scared and not sure if you are doing things right. I think I have attended to areas in my life in a different way than I did before being a mom. I learned a lot about fear and facing fear. I do feel like a more fully developed woman as a mom. I feel like I physically take better care of myself, my mind and my spirit, all of it." She does yoga, eats healthy foods, and strives to find a healthy balance in her life.

I didn't expect to be a mom
of an only child.

Being a mom to an only child has its joys and challenges for Jasmine. "I didn't expect to be a mom of an only child. And there are things that are great about that, and things that are challenging about that. There isn't a built-in playmate around, and so he sometimes needs a lot of attention." The advantage of having only one child for Jasmine is that, "I feel like I can really focus my attention on him." She remembered thinking when her son was born, "I don't have any more love, and I couldn't possibly love another child, which I know was not true."

Jasmine describes her son as having "a lot of energy. He is very curious, and kind of into everything. Especially when he was a toddler, you had to have your eyes on him at all times. You turn your back and he would be in the closet dumping out a bottle of bleach or something. It was just amazing. All things that will serve him well as an adult but they are really challenging, but they are getting less as he gets older." "He has now been diagnosed with Attention Deficit Hyperactivity Disorder (ADHD), which I feel like we always knew, but we didn't start testing until later. He could just be kind of naughty, especially in family situations. I could see the eye rolling and that was a challenge. That was embarrassing and really stressful for me. I think when I was married one of the challenges was that his dad and I have very different parenting styles. So I was the bad guy because I was more strict. I hated that feeling."

I feel more rested, more patient,
and able to deal with him and parent him
more gently and effectively.

There have been many good things that have resulted from their new family dynamic. "We [she and her ex-husband] have a very amicable relationship and we went through a mediation process that took a long time. It was never like 'I hate you, I need a divorce from you right now.'" Jasmine and her husband share custody, with their son going back and forth every 3 days. "There is something to be said about having him to myself and when I am with him, I am with him, and when I am not with him, that is when I do everything else. Not that I would have wanted a divorce to make that happen, but I feel more rested, more patient, and able to deal with him and parent him more gently and effectively now that I get those breaks."

*I accept him more
for who he is.*

Although it has been challenging in the last several years, dealing with a separation, divorce, and working to mitigate some behavior issues associated with her son's Attention Deficit Disorder, Jasmine and her son have a good relationship. "I think I accept him more for who he is." She has started enjoying more of the traits in her son that used to be frustrating. "He loves guns and stuff like that and I hate that stuff. I was like 'my kid is not playing with guns,' but its something you can't really control because anything can turn into a gun. Now he is kind of a mama's boy. He is very sweet to me. I think he has gotten a little easier. I feel more joy. I like being with him. I like doing stuff with him. I just have more quality time with him, although it has been hard and not what anybody really expected. I feel like my relationship with him is better now."

Jasmine feels fortunate to have the support of friends and family. "I have a couple of friends who have older kids who I really respect as moms. I feel like I can talk to them and they know what I mean, they get it." They give Jasmine gentle encouragement and affirmations like, "You are a great mom." "I think my dad has given me a lot of support too. It is so weird to see him as a grandpa, and he is way more gentle with the grandkids, but he still has those expectations too. He is just very much a patriarch. Ryan just loves his papa."

*I ask him 'how does your body feel?'
I try to help him get in touch
with his feelings and emotions.*

After becoming a mother, Jasmine developed a desire to have a connection to some form of spirituality. "I really wanted Ryan to have a spiritual community and so we were going to a Unitarian church for a while; it is not so much based around religion, because I was "anti" religion for many years. He asks about God and Jesus. I feel comfortable talking to him about it. I do a lot of yoga so that is the mind-body connection stuff. I talk to him about that and I ask him 'how does your body feel?' I try to help him get in touch with his feelings and emotions."

"I want him to know a lot about different faiths and I want him to make that decision when he wants." Jasmine is committed to keep an open dialogue with her son about spirituality and talks to him about it regularly. "Even though he doesn't go to church every week, he's getting bits and pieces. His dad does a lot of meditation and studies Buddhism, so it is touching his life. I feel much more open and realized how important it was to me right away, right after I had him. I'm definitely more spiritual since becoming a mom."

I think I am a pretty good mom
but I have a lot of self-doubts.

When asked how she would describe herself as a mother, Jasmine said, "I think I am strict and can come off harsh sometimes. I think that is the thing that I struggle with the most because he is such a sensitive boy. But I know that I am loving. I know that I can come back and say, 'I'm sorry, Mom didn't mean to yell at you,' or whatever. Without spoiling him I try and give him what he needs, and wants, not so much in terms of things, but opportunities and experiences. I feel like I am open and I tell him that he can talk to me about anything. I also know that I can get so stressed out and feel overwhelmed with him sometimes. I think I am a pretty good mom but I have a lot of self-doubts."

Jasmine finds herself enjoying being a mother more and more as her son gets older, and she is able to embrace the difficulties they have in a more positive light. "I think I accept him more for who he is. It's like okay, you got exactly the opposite of what you thought you were going to get, what you wanted to get, but he is a great kid. If he knows when he is grown up that his dad and I always did the best that we could, that he was loved, then I just feel like that's what it is all about, that he would know how much he is loved."

The Fifth Sacred Question

Am I ready to let go?

Contemplate your pregnancy, birth, and motherhood experiences, and how your early expectations compare to what your real lived experience has been.

- How has motherhood fulfilled your expectations?
- What has surprised you?
- How have you been disappointed?
- What has been even better than you expected?
- Is there anything that is frustrating or upsetting you?
- Do you have concerns and worries?
- Are you trying to control the situation?
- What ideas or assumptions are you clinging to?
- Is there something you are resisting?
- Are you ready to release the hurt?
- What would be most helpful?
- Do you have supportive family and friends?

- Can you accept life as the imperfectly perfect experience that it is?
- Can you release the idea that you must be perfect to be a good mother?
- Are you ready to forgive yourself and others for being human?
- What stage of motherhood has been the most difficult for you?
- Are you living for today or dwelling on yesterday?
- Do you want to make peace with your past?
- What about the future excites you?
- Can you enjoy life as it is?
- Are you ready to let go?

Am I ready to let go?

Bridget's Story

She is my everything.
There is nothing in the world that matters
more than my child.
—Bridget

Bridget became a mother when she was 34 years old. "I knew what I was going to name her. We all had our little 'Team Rachel' nametags on for the hospital." Bridget organized a group of dedicated friends that would be supporting her in the birthing process. "I am a solo mother by choice and I really hate hospitals. I did not want to be there ever, ever, ever. The deal was I was not to be left alone ever in the hospital." She also created a birth plan. "I had written the whole birth plan ahead of time and that was really important to me because I did not want any men touching me. I felt completely vulnerable and did not want to be in a hospital setting."

I woke up with this feeling like a freight train
was going through my belly.

Bridget's due date was June 1st, but her daughter surprised everyone by coming several weeks early. "Actually my water broke at the baby shower my friend was having for me, and I was embarrassed because I thought, 'Oh God, did I pee my pants?' I'm sitting on her chair. My friend said, 'it's okay, don't worry about it; maybe your water broke?'" After being checked at the hospital, Bridget went home with her housemate Abby, because she was not having any cramps or contractions. "About 3:30 in the morning I woke up with this feeling like a freight train was going through my belly." She and Abby raced to the hospital. "I was supposed to have a water tub or birthing tub and they couldn't get the water into the tub. This is a major hospital; this is why I went to this hospital, to be able to have this experience I wanted."

Everything that Bridget had learned about labor did not come close to the actual experience of how it felt for her. "I was screaming the whole time, and people are looking at me." Bridget's plan to have her baby in the birthing tub, however, did not happen as she had hoped it would. "It was like Chinese water drip torture because I could see the tub and they were not filling it. They had this huge tub to fill and they weren't getting anything but drips of water in." Instead of giving birth in a tub filled with water, Bridget was sent to the shower, and then she was up on a table. "And for someone who wanted a natural childbirth there I was indeed begging for drugs. They said to me, 'You can't have them.' It was not pretty; there were not any happy, blissful moments of having a gentle birth. I was a screaming animal saying, 'Get this thing out of me because I'm being ripped apart.' I seriously would have killed people because it was like, 'you don't mess with me.' I am a mama bear all the way."

> *All the pain that had been so intense,*
> *it was like a switch that flipped*
> *to this intense joy.*

Upset, in pain, feeling quite neglected by the hospital staff, and disappointed about the birthing tub, Bridget gave birth to her daughter after 2 hours of hard labor. "When she looked me right in my eyes I heard her say, 'Oh there you are mama, I've been wondering what you look like. I've been waiting to meet you this whole time.'" In an instant everything changed for Bridget. "All the pain that had been so intense, it was like a switch that flipped to this intense joy. It was like being struck by a bolt of lightning and that freight train had vanished."

Birth is sacred.
It is not to be taken lightly.

Although Bridget's birth experience could be described as a successful event in that her baby was born without drugs, and there were no complications, there were many things about it that greatly disappointed and upset Bridget. "I was very upset that I did not get to have my midwife that I had through the pregnancy. I had to deal with whoever was on call." Understanding there are staffing challenges, Bridget still felt this was unacceptable. "If we really had respect for women you would have your birth provider, whether that is your midwife or your doctor, plus your doula if you want one. You don't just go to somebody else, whoever is on duty that night." She is adamant that women should be treated better when they are having a baby. "Birth is way too important for that. It is the most intense spiritual experience I have probably ever had, in a mix of the spiritual and physical sense experience. Birth is sacred. It is not to be taken lightly." During pregnancy and childbirth, Bridget was continually impressed with her body. "It is such a powerful human experience to birth this life."

Having your own baby
is a love that is beyond anything.

When Bridget went home after giving birth the surprises continued. "I discovered that I had no idea what I was in for. Everything that I thought I knew, what it would be like while I was pregnant, everything that I had put in my head about what motherhood was going to be like, it was just so much more. Yes, I knew I would love my baby, and I loved her when I was pregnant, and all that, but I had no idea what love was until she was born." Despite being in romantic relationships all her life, the bond she felt with her new baby girl was different. "Having your own baby is a love that is beyond anything."

Bridget breastfed her baby, and had read all about it when she was pregnant. "But the reading didn't compare to the actual lived experience of nursing this baby. I was completely blown away by the fact that my body can produce food." A fierce protectiveness came over Bridget for her new little baby. Her beloved cat was given away to a new home, and her prominent career at the state capitol no longer felt as important to her.

Bridget's career and motherhood proved to be a challenging combination. Her boss, despite being a single mom herself, was not willing to give Bridget much time off. "She thought I should be back to work at three weeks, at least part-time. I tried to go back to work and I absolutely hated it. I didn't want to be there and I was just miserable. I wanted my baby."

No one was going to tell me
I couldn't nurse my baby.

When her baby was just 6 months old, Bridget had to attend a weeklong convention for work. A friend that was going to help watch her baby got sick, and Bridget's beloved aunt, who was also there to help, had limited mobility. "I had to have Rachel with me. I didn't think it was a big problem to nurse her. I had my back turned to everybody. My boss wanted me to be at the registration desk. No one even had to come up to the desk and look at her." Bridget's boss did not approve of the situation. "My boss ripped me a new one in front of everybody for nursing my baby in public. She said, 'you could take her in the bathroom.' I said, 'I'm not nursing my baby in a bathroom stall, that is where people poop. Not happening. I'm not teaching my baby to be ashamed of wanting to eat.' No one was going to tell me I couldn't nurse my baby. I mean there are women's breasts everywhere, in news media, popping out of teeny-weeny bikinis, breasts are used to sell everything, but my breasts which are making food for my baby are somehow now taboo. She was six months old and she wanted to nurse and she's going to nurse."

I didn't take on the shame
that she was trying to give me
because there just was no shame.

Bridget, used to being an advocate and defending others, chose to not engage her boss, and instead remained calm and kept her cool. "In that moment, it's like something washed over me that I didn't have to be the one who was ashamed. I didn't take on the shame that she was trying to give me because there just was no shame." That was the day Bridget decided she needed to leave. "I think it was one of the hardest times of my life because I am so used to being an advocate for other people and jumping up to defend, and it was this thing of letting it go." That experience solidified a dawning realization about her new priorities as a mother. "I knew what was most important, and it was not the job."

"The real kicker for me came one day when I was leaving the capitol to go to my car to pick her up from daycare, and it was always a rush. The rush to get her there, to nurse her first, and get her up and dressed and diapered and ready to go, and me up and dressed and presentable, and to get her to daycare by 7:30 so I could be to work by 8:00. This is terribly stressful. I am not a morning person. Maybe it is stressful even for morning people. Every day was a struggle. Then the struggle to be done and be there on time, by 5:30, to pick her up."

There is nothing in the world
that matters more than my child.

On that day, rushing out of the capitol after work, a woman in an SUV almost hit Bridget as she stepped out to cross the road. "She totally, completely smashed my aura, but she didn't physically touch me." Bridget started screaming and went into a panic. "I've got this baby who needs me. I don't have a family of origin that I wanted anywhere near her. Even my beloved aunt, there was no way she could raise this baby. I couldn't imagine my baby living without me." It felt like a wake-up call for Bridget. "I am her food source. She is my world. She is my everything. There is nothing in the world that matters more than my child." With some help from security, Bridget calmed down, got to her car, and went to pick up her daughter at daycare. "I saw her and just sobbed and sobbed."

When Bridget was able to secure health insurance (a big factor), Bridget found shared office space and started her own private practice, specializing in family law. This turned out to be a wonderful fit with motherhood. "I have been able to work from home much of the time. The others in the office were really good when Rachel was little; I always brought her with me when I needed to go to work. I would bring her to check the mail and check e-mail and set things up, but most of my work I could do from home when she was sleeping or when I had arranged play dates." That was 11 years ago. "I am so glad I did it because it has given me time to be with my daughter. Financially, if you looked at it on paper on a balance sheet, you would say, 'you are crazy, don't leave this job where you had all this potential and you are earning the most money you've ever earned in your life.' What I learned is that professionally, I didn't really care so much about being a lawyer as much as I cared about being a mother."

As a staunch feminist and lesbian, Bridget describes herself as "outspoken, very opinionated and very protective" of her daughter. "She is a gorgeous redhead with long curly hair. I used to say if I had a dollar for everyone who commented on her hair I would have diapers and daycare paid for." Bridget became frustrated with all the comments about her daughter's hair when she was little. "I was constantly saying, 'She's got a great big brain underneath that hair.'" She encourages her daughter to develop critical-thinking skills, especially about women's issues, and about the decisions she makes in her life. "She knows that we don't go to Wal-Mart, and we don't watch Disney movies (except Brave, it was an exception because the character had red hair and it's a mother daughter movie, but she was still way too skinny, her and her mother)."

*There are many
different kinds of families.*

When her daughter was little, Bridget was creative in how she helped her daughter learn that there are many different kinds of families. "The norm for most of the kids in our Early Childhood and Family Education (ECFE) class was having two moms." When her daughter went to school she attended a Spanish immersion school that has a large amount of ethnic diversity. "It has been the norm for her. And it is a norm that she just has a mom." Even when her daughter was little Bridget took it upon herself to alter the stories she read to her daughter. "I also changed all the characters in the kid's books from male to female because I just could not stand it. So many of the good roles in books went to boys." Some people ask Bridget if her daughter wants a dad. "Actually, she has never expressed any real interest in that." Bridget has taught her daughter to be proud, and never ashamed, of her family.

In addition, Bridget created a family of close friends with lots of "grandmas" for her daughter, and they belong to a women's spirituality group. Bridget found them when she was exploring her spirituality in her 20's. Her first meeting with them was in a park outside. "They were honoring this tree, not worshipping in that sense, but honoring the tree and honoring nature, and honoring the gifts of the tree, and showing respect. I had found my tribe. It was wonderful. Of course I wanted to share this with my daughter." They have been a wonderful source of support for Bridget as a solo mother, and the women adore her daughter. "We had her at summer solstice since she was 6 weeks. We had her blessing ceremony. It was amazing to me that I had the support of this group. Rachel has been their little darling."

Breast milk is the ultimate comfort food.
When your child is upset, you want to comfort them.
That is what you do.

Creating rituals and celebrating milestones in her daughter's life is important to Bridget. One of those moments was when Bridget stopped nursing her daughter as her daughter turned 5. "We had a whole ritual that I had planned, her growing up ritual." Neither Bridget nor her daughter wanted to end nursing, so the ritual was meant for both of them in some ways. "We were going to have our final nursing in the circle surrounded by the ones we love." Her daughter got to help plan it so it was not just done for her, so she could talk about the way she was growing up and all the good things that she could now do by herself, things that she could enjoy. "We had the ceremony in the park, and everything was great, and mama got her tears out for the last nursing."

Even though her daughter did nurse one more time, their special ritual marked the end of nursing for Bridget and her daughter. Bridget was proud to have nursed her daughter, and did not let anything stop her, not even the painful experience of getting one of her breasts caught in a mixer when she was making a cake at a friend's house for her daughter's first birthday. "The mixer caught my shirt and kept going." It was moment in motherhood that Bridget will never forget. "I am screaming. Rachel is screaming and the dogs are barking." Despite that unfortunate incident, Bridget kept nursing. "I would have never believed I would have done it for five years but it was the best thing we ever did. She had so few health problems, and as a solo mom it was something that really bonded us; it was a special closeness that we had. Knowing that I could always comfort her, because yes, breast milk is the ultimate comfort food. When your child is upset, you want to comfort them. That is what you do."

One of the most important experiences Bridget is proud to give her daughter is the Michigan Women's

Music Festival. "I made a commitment, we are not missing Michigan, she is going every year of her life if I have to strap her to the top of the car and she gets bugs in her teeth, we're going." The festival is an all-women, all-girl environment.

The first year of taking her daughter to the festival was a difficult transition for Bridget. "So here I am and I have this baby at festival and I am used to being able to go off and do whatever I want whenever I want, stay out as late as I want, and now I am completely tied down and having to cope with that. It was a huge adjustment. It was not easy at all. Here I was at the place where I have the most freedom and now feeling the most restricted, and I have no help. I couldn't even go to the 'Porta-Jane' by myself. What do you do with a tiny baby that you can't set down? I'm managing everything like keeping my baby from being sunburned. I had to keep her cool during the day when it was hot. I had to keep her warm at night when it gets cold."

Bridget found special help from a Canadian woman named Pat. "Pat took it upon herself that I was her charge and this little Rachel was her family too, and so she gave me a night out where I could go out and do something fun. So I got one night to go out and dance. She is a little older than me and she was just so helpful and really was the support that I needed." Bridget also noticed that she got only warm smiles and nods of encouragement at festival from the other women when she nursed her daughter, even when she was no longer an infant, and none of the judgmental looks and frowns like she did back home.

Now that her daughter is older, Bridget allows her to go around festival with her friends and she has a lot of freedom, a freedom that she does not have in the regular world. "That saddens me because my childhood growing up was completely outdoors. We lived about a mile out of town and had a horse and had trees to climb and things to do. In the summertime you were outside from the moment you got up to when you went to bed." At least her daughter can have that experience at festival. "That to me is the biggest gift I can give her—to have that independence that she can't get anywhere else, and to know she is as safe as she can be."

Despite the challenges of being a solo mother, Bridget would not change it for anything. "I feel very fortunate actually because I am a solo mother by choice." In her work with family law, she deals with many divorces. "My clients' experiences have taught me that it can be a living hell." She witnesses many women coming to the table after having done all the work of raising the children when they were little only to have to agree to share their kids with the father because the father does not want to pay as much in child support. Seeing these kinds of situations that women are in makes Bridget thankful. "I shoulder a heavy burden, but I am really glad that I don't have to share that."

I think one of the hardest things
is doing the working mom routine.

Making a living and being a mother is a difficult combination however. "I think one of the hardest things is doing the working mom routine. The challenge has been trying to figure out how to both earn a living and be a parent, and a parent in a meaningful way." For Bridget, that meant not taking her to daycare and working full time. She did not want to miss any of her daughter's milestones; she wanted to be there for everything.

Bridget really wanted and loves having a daughter. "I wouldn't have anything else. We were meant to be together in this lifetime. It is very clear to me that she chose me to be her mother and I tell her that I thank Goddess for her every day. I say to her, 'I am so glad you chose me to be your mama.' Because in my view, she did."

> *You have to challenge things*
> *because nothing is going to change*
> *unless you do.*

Most important to Bridget, she wants her daughter to learn her values. "I want for her to have my spiritual values but yet the tricky part is my spiritual values include that I don't get to force anybody into doing anything that they don't want to do." She wants her daughter to think independently and know she does not have to accept everything that is pushed in our society. She wants her daughter to know "that you have to challenge things because nothing is going to change unless you do."

Bridget knows her daughter will get to make her own choices about her life. "My guess is she might have to rebel a little bit." Bridget is okay with that. She does not want her daughter to succumb to authority without question, and go along with what everybody else is doing. "If there is one thing I can do as a mother it is to be able to cause her to think first." Bridget knows that everything that is important to her may not be what is important to her daughter, but she is hoping that as she grows up she will value all the wonderful things that she got to experience and learn with her mother.

The Sixth Sacred Question

What is most important to me?

Your values and priorities determine what is most important to you.

Your Values = *the things that are important to you*

Your Priorities = *determined by your values*

Values + Priorities = *How you spend your time, money, energy, How you behave, how you relate to others*

Contemplate the following questions.

- How did your priorities change when you became a mother?
- What is most important to you as a mother right now?
- As a mother, what are you most proud of?
- What gives you the most fulfillment at this stage of motherhood?

- What values do you want to impress upon your children?

- Do you feel good about yourself as a mother? Why or why not?

- If you could change one thing about motherhood, what would it be?

- How are you the same as your mother?

- How are you different than your mother?

- Do you have a healthy balance in your life between work and home, and between caring for others and nourishing your self?

- If you had more time and money, how would you spend it?

- Do you and your partner share similar values and priorities?

- If your life does not reflect your values and priorities, what do you need to change?

- Do you belong to a community that shares your values?

What is most important to me?

Lexie's Story

I am so grateful for the shared bond
I have with other mothers...
—Lexie

Lexie had her first child when she was 27 years old. "I actually think I first became a mother when I was pregnant with a pregnancy that ended in a miscarriage, before Kayla was born. With that baby, I started to really feel like a mother: when I found out I was pregnant and then even giving birth through miscarriage. I think of that baby as my first child still. And that really was a change in many ways. It sent me into a lot of depression, having lost that child. I spent about a year and a half in a depression that I didn't even recognize until I came out of it. I think that is often the case with depression; you don't recognize it in the middle of it. I came out of it part way through my pregnancy with Kayla. I felt like I was coming back to life with the baby that was in me."

I, as many people do,
had a picture of motherhood
that shattered the minute Kayla was born.

Lexie was in labor for a long time with her daughter. "She had somewhat of a traumatic birth. It was a long labor and I was exhausted. As she was coming out, my husband said the midwife just basically grabbed and yanked on her." Lexie's daughter was born healthy but she cried a lot, which was upsetting for Lexie, but not for her husband. "In the hospital, she was screaming and the nurses were coming down the hall and he (my husband) was just sleeping. That was really frustrating. And she would not sleep lying down ever, not even in my arms or next to me. In order to sleep she needed to be upright. So I spent the first four months of her life carrying her upright for untold hours of the night. I, as many people do, had a picture of motherhood that shattered the minute Kayla was born."

Lexie came from a family that had given her a natural framework for motherhood. "I came from a family that breastfed, and did attachment parenting. And breastfeeding was supposed to solve everything. Put a baby to the breast and they are supposed to get happy. She never did. She only wanted to nurse for food, not for comfort, and from about the time she was born she screamed, for 8-12 hours a day, which was hard. It was really hard. It was not the introduction to motherhood I had expected." In hindsight, Lexie believes her daughter's traumatic birth was the cause of her constant crying. "I am convinced her spine was out of line. She was in pain if she was lying down."

From about the time she was born
she screamed,
for 8-12 hours a day.

Lexie was fortunate to have help from her parents when her daughter was a baby. Her parent's house had become contaminated with a chemical and they had to move out for a while. "We had an apartment above our house and they moved in there." Lexie was able to get some sleep while her mother carried the baby around. "That was the most amazing thing. Really, it made me realize that I couldn't do it all alone, which is a great thing to realize in the first four weeks of mothering."

I had wanted so much to be a mother
that it was still good even when it was hard.

Having her parents so close by helped Lexie survive the first days and weeks at home with her fussy baby. "My Dad was gone to work during the days, but my Mom was able to be there. And in so many ways I was blessed to have her. In many ways it was really hard having my mom there when I was a new mom, because I didn't necessarily want to do everything just the way she did. But I was so blessed to have that support and that ability to hand off the baby to someone for an hour and sleep when I really needed to. I wouldn't have been able to sleep through her screaming. If I laid her down she would have been screaming. It was hard." Although it was challenging to have such a fussy baby, Lexie was steadfast in her desire to be a mother. "We got through it. I stayed sane. I had wanted so much to be a mother that it was still good even when it was hard. It was like this is what I wanted. I'm here. We're going to get through. It'll get better. I convinced myself of that. And I was right. It got better." Lexie reflects back on her first days and months with her daughter and says it actually helped her with the next two babies. "When walking the one night I would remember that I used to walk the floor every night. I'd know I could get through this. The other two seemed very easy after Kayla."

Shortly after becoming a mother, Lexie felt the personal awareness of how much her role as a mother changed her daily life. "Even if I could give Kayla to someone else for a little while, she was totally dependent on me. She was dependent on me for food, for comforting her, if there was something wrong, whatever was making her scream, I was responsible for trying to figure it out and make it better, or if I couldn't, for letting her know I was trying to make it better. She was totally dependent on me for all of it. Even though I had done a lot of caring for children before that, it was never 24/7 with no end in sight. And so that changed, even if it was expected, it was the sudden realization of the reality of this responsibility. Yes, someone else might be willing to take care of her for a little while, but this was primarily my job now."

> *Suddenly my relationship with my husband,*
> *Charles, changed very dramatically.*

Lexie's marriage was also impacted by having a baby, and by all the responsibilities that go along with parenting. "Suddenly my relationship with my husband, Charles, changed very dramatically. I got resentful because he was not picking her up when she cried, or volunteering at all to help take care of the baby. And that didn't resolve until my second child was born. Then suddenly it was, 'okay, I can't care for both of them 100% of the time anymore. If they are both screaming at bedtime, you now need to help.' I feel like he didn't take on the role of fathering until that time, three years later, after I had taken on the role of full-time mothering." By the time Lexie had her third baby, her husband had assumed an active parenting role. "The fact that we have been co-parenting now, much more so than at the beginning, has strengthened our relationship in a lot of ways."

Friendships with other mothers became a wonderful source of support for Lexie. "Suddenly, having a child opened up a whole new world of people to meet. If you don't have kids, it can be really hard to meet people. But suddenly I had other mothers as friends, which was nice." Lexie made friends with a mother who also gave birth with her midwife, and she found other mothers who valued breastfeeding through La Leche League. "Making those connections was wonderful, connections with those who had similar parenting philosophies. Those changes were really positive ones for me."

> *There are resources within me*
> *that I didn't know were there,*
> *until I had to draw on them to keep going*
> *when I didn't think I could.*

Lexie has chosen to be a stay-at-home mom to her children, and has devoted herself to homeschooling them as well. She describes herself as being a pretty flexible and persistent mom, even though she has found she is not as patient as she once thought she was. "I can keep at it; I can keep walking the floor for a long, long time, longer than I think I can if I just keep going. There are resources within me that I didn't know were there, until I had to draw on them to keep going when I didn't think I could, to keep picking up a screaming child even when all I wanted to do was throw a blanket over my head and go to sleep, that depth, that ability to keep going, I would not have known was there."

> *I love it when everyone*
> *is all snuggled together at night.*

Lexie also describes herself as, "Connected; that might be the most important word to describe me as a mother. I am connected with my children. Keeping the connection, knowing their interests, knowing what they need, trying to meet the needs and navigate the wants. Really, it is about making that connection…I really feel fulfilled by being a mother and I think it is partly because there are connections here that I can really influence so much. I have managed, so far, to keep them good. I enjoy little things like cuddling a lot. I am a physically expressive person. I like cuddling with the kids. I love it when everyone is all snuggled together at night."

Being a stay-at-home mom for Lexie meant finding a balance of being at home with her children and getting out of the house and being socially active for her own well-being. She realized after having children that she was more extroverted than she thought. "I discovered I really needed to find ways to talk with adults on a regular basis, maybe not daily, but really close." While her parents were living with Lexie she was able to visit with her mother on a daily basis, but after they moved back into their own house Lexie did not have that built-in social network anymore. "I realized about then that I needed to be doing things that brought me into conversations and contact with other people." Not being out in the workplace meant Lexie had to be proactive and intentional in finding ways to make connections outside the home. She joined a "buying club," became a La Leche League and 4-H Leader, and became involved at her local health food cooperative. It was important to Lexie to find organizations that are child-friendly. "They are all activities that I can bring my children to, or able to be rescheduled if I need to because of the needs of my children."

I walk next door,
so I can see her
and make that connection.

Part of Lexie's long-term solution to making sure she has the social network she needs to be happy and healthy was to buy the house that came up for sale next to one of her good friends. "The best part of the move is that anytime I feel like I need that connection I can walk next door. I can come up with something I need to ask her. And I rarely call her, I walk next door, so I can see her and make that connection. She is one of my mothering mentors. Her youngest is the age of my oldest. Having a mentor living next door is wonderful. It really is."

Her friend and mentor is a great source of inspiration for Lexie. "Just having that calm presence, that example right there, reminds me, oh yeah, that's what I want to be. I can works toward it. And I know no one is perfect, she yells at her kids too sometimes. But again even seeing that, the way she then apologizes and reconnects. I go, oh yeah, we can reconnect even when it is not going right. Because it never goes right all the time." Being a mother has brought many close friendships with other women into Lexie's life. "I am so grateful for the shared bond I have with other mothers, especially other mothers who have similar beliefs and values, those connections."

One of Lexie's core values is having a healthy lifestyle for her family, and as a result she got involved with a community that shares her values. "Again, I connected with people I had met because we were mothers and were all wanting to get the chemicals out of our children's lives. Eating organically was a priority because of the kids as much as for ourselves. Also, finding other natural products, alternatives to plastic, avoiding BPA and other chemicals, that kind of thing. All of that came with being a mom." Lexie reached out to other parents in the community and became someone they could go to for advice. "I've been organic gardening since I was four. I have a lot of knowledge and resources that I have had for a long time."

My four-year-olds favorite color
right now is pink.
He's got pink boots and he loves them.

Being a mother to a girl and two boys has made Lexie aware of the large amount of gender bias that still exists in our society. Her concern today is more for her sons than her daughter. "If a little girl wants to play with little boy toys, it might seem unusual to some people, but overall, its fine. But if you go in and you want dolls and pink pretty little puppy things, if you are buying those for your son, people are going to wonder about that." Lexie has chosen to ignore the dominant stereotypes for boys and girls. "My four-year-olds favorite color right now is pink. He's got pink boots and he loves them. People find it hard to believe that and they see his boots and they think that he's a girl. Girls can be just like little boys in the way they dress and what they play with, but boys can't be anything like little girls really. It's just not socially acceptable."

From Lexie's perspective as a mother, gender bias is at least as much of a problem for boys as for girls. "So girls have come ahead, now we have to do something so boys know they can be caring and that its okay to show emotions, and that pink isn't only for girls." Because her middle son had ringlet curls, people often mistook him for a girl. "At some point I decided it wasn't such a horrible thing that people thought he was a little girl, because they were so much gentler. It's been a pretty amazing discovery." This realization has made Lexie much more aware of how she interacts with boys and girls in her various leadership roles in the community. "I don't think I would have known that if I hadn't had both boys and a girl."

She is also aware of the cultural messages that her daughter is exposed to as she gets older, and tries to shield her as much as possible from advertising that objectifies women or emphasizes the importance of a woman's appearance. "I try to help her know that is not where her value is. It doesn't come from how she looks physically because that still tends to be so much of our culture." Lexie has easily accepted the bodily changes that have taken place as a result of having three children. "I don't have the type of body that is considered ideal in our culture, no matter what I did, I never would. I came to terms with that long before I had children." Lexie is doing her best to teach her daughter about having a healthy body image as she moves into her adolescent years.

I really need quiet
for thirty seconds please
so I can think.

Some of the challenges Lexie deals with as a mother to three children are about creating healthy boundaries and finding ways to balance all the conflicting needs at any given time. "Reconciling the different needs, whether they are the needs that I have or that my children have or that my husband has, or the pressure put on us by the outside world. There are a lot of ways that meeting needs and trying to reconcile them can be hard. Even before putting your own needs into the picture. Sometimes I think, 'I really need quiet for thirty seconds please so I can think of a solution.' But it rarely happens that I'll have the time to think." Along with balancing everyone's needs, Lexie realizes she cannot always shield and protect her children from getting hurt. "The other hard part about mothering is dealing with those scary things that happen to your kids that make you feel helpless, without letting the fear take hold."

When Lexie reflects on what has contributed to her positive experiences in motherhood she said, "Really wanting to be a mom, and having the support—I think those are the two top things. They are both really important." Even if being a mother didn't go the way she expected at the beginning, Lexie still knew, "this is what I wanted to do." Lexie also feels the support she has from other mothers, and her and her husband's families, has been critical in her ability to get through the hard times.

Challenges are going to be there,
and so I might as well decide to enjoy them.

Lexie remembers reading her mothers "Mothering" magazines from the time she was seven years old through her early years as a mother, and feels that it helped her learn about motherhood before she actually became a mother. "That support too of constantly reading stories. They often published not just things that were going great, but also the challenges of mothering. It helped knowing in advance that I wasn't necessarily in for all golden days, smiles, and a baby that was happy in my arms. Being prepared in advance for some of the realities of mothering helped too. Even if I did think that breastfeeding should fix everything, I knew that babies cry a lot. I knew there were going to be challenges." Lexie keeps in mind an old saying that helps her get through the difficult stages of childrearing, "this too shall pass." "I am enjoying the challenges. Daily I am making a decision to do so, those challenges are going to be there, and so I might as well decide to enjoy them."

7

The Seventh Sacred Question

Where is my circle of support?

Contemplate the following questions:

- Who, in your life, is positive, encouraging, and trustworthy?
- Are your friends there for you when you need them?
- Who are the women that you admire and look up to? Why?
- Do you take time to nurture your bonds of friendship?
- Who can you talk to about issues in your life?
- Do you regularly laugh and cry and have fun with other women?
- Who would you like to spend more time with?
- What kind of friend do you want to be to other women?

Write a letter, Make a Phone Call

Today, think of someone who has been supportive to you as a mother. Take time to write a letter of appreciation and gratitude, or call to say "thank you." Honor what they have given you. Think of the smile on their face when they read your words or hear your voice. What a lovely gift.

Where is my circle of support?

Bella's Story

"I think being aware of how to make your marriage
happy and executing on those things is super important."
—Bella

Bella was 26 years old when she had her first child. She chose to have a natural birth, including no medication for pain. "You can prepare for the pain but it's very challenging to go through. I remember my husband and my doula being right there by my side." Once she was in labor, the experience became intense. "I remember thinking that women all over the world do this. This is crazy." The birth experience took on a surreal quality for Bella. "Just feeling the moment she came out, and then the pain subsided almost immediately. I was thinking that I could do anything in the world. There's no challenge that I could not surmount because I just did this incredibly painful thing, this task that I really had no idea that my body could endure."

Giving birth, without pain medication was a powerful experience for Bella. "I wish I could just bottle up that feeling. There are some feelings you wish you could just put in a bottle and then take a pill to recall that feeling of being invincible, like I could do anything, because I had just done this amazing thing." Bella felt the singularity of her purpose in giving birth, but also the support of those around her. "My husband and my doula have no idea what I am going through right now, but they are here with me. For this long moment I felt so alone in that, but also together. The baby comes and I remember spending quite a bit of time with her and nursing at the hospital and just thinking that this was a new life."

I was unprepared
for what motherhood
brought to my life.

Bringing home her baby girl meant some big changes for Bella. Her normal routines had to be adjusted to accommodate a new baby. "I was unprepared for what motherhood brought to my life." Bella was used to having extreme order in her life. "When my house is not orderly my life is not orderly." Having a baby meant Bella had a new normal, one that was not as predictable as before. "You can't anticipate a lot of things about a child's day, and also the stuff, all the stuff they bring, organizing that and keeping it orderly." Bella's challenge in motherhood became about creating balance between taking care of her child's needs and taking care of her own needs. At the time she had her first child she was in graduate school and was not able to take much time off after her baby was born. She remembers it being a very busy time. "Sometimes my husband would meet me at the school so I could nurse."

You've got to make your life work
with all the things you have in it,
and you've got to figure out a way to do that.

Bella knew she was going into a field that was demanding and wondered how women make it all work.

"How can you have a successful career and have kids?" Other women who had older children were reassuring but shared her concern. "I remember talking to people about that and they were like, yeah, it gets easier." Trying to find a healthy and happy balance between work, school and motherhood was new territory for Bella. "I think I discovered that for the first time I felt like, I don't know how to do this." She felt a deep sense of responsibility in motherhood that was different than anything she had experienced before in high school or college. "That was really a major learning experience for me. Even now I feel that way. You've got to make your life work with all the things you have in it, and you've got to figure out a way to do that."

Three years after their first daughter was born, Bella had another baby girl. Again, she used a doula and had a natural childbirth with no pain medications. Bella and her family were now living in Florida where Bella had a challenging new job. When the job ended Bella finally had time to explore the city they lived in. "Several times I took my older daughter who was five at the time to do really fun city things. We went to museums, and walked around downtown, and had pizza at this amazing pizza place, where there is this famous chef. I took her out of school, and I had the other one in school. We just bummed around, like mother-daughter bumming around, and it was really fun."

*I do enjoy being one-on-one
with my kids.*

Bella discovered how much she relishes these special moments alone with her daughters. "I do enjoy being one-on-one with my kids, like taking them out for hot chocolate, or having pizza together, one-on-one." Taking time to hang out and chat with her daughters as they grow up is important to Bella. "I strive to be a good communicator with them, and communicate on a fairly adult and mature level. I think that as they grow older it will be something I have laid the foundation for. I hope we can grow as women in the way we communicate with each other."

*I had more energy
to commit to my own life
and therefore my kids.*

After completing her job, she and her family decided to take some time off and travel. They visited Bella's family in India, and traveled to other places they had always wanted to visit, like Jamaica. While living in Jamaica for a few months, away from the stress of work, Bella had time to reflect deeply on what she wanted in her life, and what motherhood meant to her. Having some time away proved to be very nourishing for her and her family. "I had more energy to commit to my own life and therefore my kids."

While traveling, Bella had time to carefully reevaluate what it means for a woman to "do it all" or "have it all." I think this last year of not working I was able to be more reflective, and now I feel that it's okay to want a little less out of life professionally. If that sacrifice is going to make my life more full in every other way, full with my being a mother and full with being a wife, and full with being a happy individual. Because in the end it really is not all about professional success, it's about having several pieces of your life that you really feel good about and make you happy, and that you enjoy."

With more time to take care of myself,
mentally and physically,
I was able to see how my well-being
is good for my whole family.

While in Jamaica, Bella had dinner one night with a woman with a high-profile career who expressed frustration and resentment about the difficulties of balancing career and family. She told Bella, "I come home from work, and the house is a disaster, there's pee on the toilet, and the kids are screaming." Bella felt sad for this woman, and recognized those feelings, knowing how hard it had been for her as well when she was working full time. "Finding a way to make life holistic is what is necessary in order to not feel that resentment and to truly feel happy. With more time to take care of myself, mentally and physically, I was able to see how my well-being is good for my whole family. That is a really important thing for me to feel happy."

For Bella, finding a healthy balance between motherhood and the rest of her life meant finding ways to honor and keep alive some of the dreams and goals that she had before becoming a mother. "I haven't surrendered to the chaos. I have not surrendered to the messy house. I sometimes envy the women that do. I know I need a clean house. I know I need order in my life, and now I have to find ways to get those things."

Becoming a mother has made Bella a more compassionate person, especially for other mothers. "I feel extreme amounts of empathy for women in general. I hold myself to these super high standards but I never judge other people, other women, how people are managing. I look at the crying toddler in Target and I just feel immense amount of understanding." Knowing how hard it can be to stay physically fit, feed your family healthy meals, and take care of little children, Bella knows well how demanding motherhood can be. "I feel like I am a really, really understanding person as a result of becoming a mother."

I feel like a mother bear.
I want to super protect them
but I want them to also be okay
and fend for themselves.

Bella was raised in a family that valued learning, academics and professional success. She also wants to impart those qualities to her children, to help them to learn how to lead successful lives. "I feel driven for myself, and I want my kids to be driven." Having her girls perform well in school academically will always be important to Bella. "I feel like a mother bear. I want to super protect them but I want them to also be okay and fend for themselves. I want to try to understand how to do that. I feel very protective of them, but also very eager for them to learn how to get what they want without me doing it for them. I think I am very loving. I think I am very fair. I generally think because I want a more orderly life that I feel stricter. Although, I do try hard to be like the loving authoritarian instead of the irrational one. I try to justify my choices with them so that how I treat them and what I ask them to do is not arbitrary, which plays into me being a very fair person."

Along with valuing academics like her parents, Bella also values exposing her children to a variety of cultures, traditions, and religions like she experienced growing up. "I was raised in a Christian Church, but my mother is Hindu so we've always gone to temples and mosques in India. I've always been interested in every religion. I am the same way with my kids. We took them to mosques when we were in India and Egypt. We take them to churches. We've been to lots of temples. So I talk to them about whatever I know about the different religions. The exposure to a variety of religions has been important to me, and it is important to me to pass that along to my kids too. If they choose to have some particular connection at some point then fine, and if they don't, that is fine too."

I want my children to find things
they enjoy doing because I think
that is really important
to being a happy person.

While there are some things that Bella has chosen to pass onto her children from her childhood, she has chosen a different approach to extracurricular activities. When Bella was growing up she invested much of her time and energy in activities that were not necessarily ones that she would have chosen on her own accord, but she felt a desire to please her parents and therefore continued doing them for many years. Now as a mother, Bella is committed to helping her daughters find their own interests as they grow up. "I want my children to find things they enjoy doing because I think that is really important to being a happy person."

Bella's mother grew up in a small rural village in India and came to the United States as an adult, establishing a successful career, and raising her family. Bella values education just like her mother, but in other ways, she feels the cultural differences between how her mother grew up and how she grew up create very different expectations as well as challenges in motherhood. "The acceptable choice in India is that you get married, and you go live in your husband's house, and you take care of your husband and his family. I don't think it was ever a shock to my mom to feel like she had to take care of her husband and her kids because that was all around her. For me, that was not how it was. My mom took care of everything. I saw her working and taking care of everything. I guess I just wasn't prepared to come into a situation where I have to take care of so many things."

It seems like all the patience and extra love is going towards raising your children.

Having a baby also had a big impact on Bella's marriage. "My husband and I had been married for seven years before we had our first child and had a really romantic and loving partnership." With first one baby, and then a second baby 3 years later, things inevitably changed for Bella and her husband. "One of the major challenges is the strain on your marriage that comes from having two little kids." She and her husband have both realized that it takes a lot of dedication to raise children and that it is not always easy to find time to get away together while the children are little. "It seems like all the patience and extra love is going towards raising your children."

This has brought a new awareness for Bella about the need to dedicate time and energy to her marriage as well. "I think being aware of how to make your marriage happy and executing on those things is super important." She looks forward to more get-aways with her husband like they used to have before they had children, and remembers their special weekends away together with fondness. "I remember describing it to someone as like having an affair with your husband. It is this amazing thing; you have no guilt about it because it is like recreating that excitement in your life, being away with that person." Many of Bella's mom friends with little children feel the same way as she does about the strain on a marriage when you have little children. "They have good men who are trying to be good fathers, trying to be good husbands. I am trying to be a good mom, putting a lot of effort into that, and am kind of resting on my laurels because my marriage is solid."

Bella is fortunate to have a network of family and friends that are good sources of support to her as a mother. "Our families really love having grandkids." After living away for a year while they were traveling, Bella looks forward to settling down near family where they will have a foundation of support nearby. As she establishes her career and creates a new home for her family, she also appreciates staying connected to her friends. "The women that are in my life that are mothers, they are busy, but they understand the challenges on an intuitive level." Bella's friends are mostly working women who are in similar stages of life, trying to balance careers with motherhood and marriage. "I feel like it is easier to connect with them because they understand."

> *I am lucky to have an amazing husband*
> *who is a great father.*
> *He loves being a dad.*

Bella is especially grateful for the support of her husband, who is active and involved in parenting their children. "I am lucky to have an amazing husband who is a great father. He loves being a dad. He's really good at it." Bella's husband has also been helpful as she tries to find a healthy balance between motherhood and other area of her life. "He encourages me to do the things that make me happy because he honestly feels that if mom is happy, then the whole house is more peaceful." Bella's driven personality and her husband's laid-back style create a complimentary framework for parenting. "He just doesn't get roused by the thousands of Legos everywhere and doesn't worry about cleaning up at the end of the day. If I ask him to, he will, but if I didn't, he wouldn't. He's been an amazing support for me, absolutely."

As a mother, Bella is committed to nourishing the bonds she has with her daughters as they grow and develop into young women. "There are not that many models of really positive relationships with girls. I don't see that. Just like when you are getting married and there are not that many models of successful marriages. There are some that are out there. I think that I have created a successful marriage, generally speaking. I hope that I would be able to do the same with my kids as they grow older. I look forward to doing things with them, like talking and walking, and just being together in a peaceful way."

The Eighth Sacred Question

How can I keep my marriage from falling apart?

It is no secret that one of the biggest strains on a marriage is having little children. The responsibilities that come with having a baby take a toll on even the best partnerships.

Reflect on where your relationship is strong and where it could use some attention.

- Do you feel close and connected to your partner?
- Do you have a strong friendship?
- Is there still passion between you?
- Do you take time for romance?
- Are you 100% committed to your relationship?
- Do you help each other with the daily responsibilities of parenting?
- What would you change about your relationship to make it better?

- Is there something you need from your partner that you're not getting?
- Are you able to communicate respectfully and honestly?
- Do you have a supportive network of family and friends?

Consider the three components to love:

Intimacy - Feeling close, connected, bonded together

Passion - Physical attraction, romance, sex

Commitment - The decision to love another, and to maintain that love

And how these three components play out in relationships:

Intimacy - Leads to friendship

Passion - Leads to being romantic lovers

Commitment - Leads to being partners in daily life

How can I keep my marriage from falling apart?

Grace's Story

I had that experience of God talking in my heart.
I was quiet enough to hear, 'don't worry;
everything is going to be okay.
It's all going to be okay.'
—Grace

G race became a mother when she was 27 years old. "It took about a year to get pregnant and it seemed like a really long year." Grace had watched her own mom enjoying motherhood. "She was a really good mom and my inspiration, so I always wanted to be a mom. I knew that forever." One of her memories from this time in her life was when she attended her church for an event and prayed with a sister. "I prayed about letting all that go, about not being able to conceive. It wasn't too long after that that I found out I was pregnant. That is actually a common theme throughout my life, feeling that God has worked in it, particularly with my children. That was the first one, and I had such tears of joy when I found out that I was pregnant." Grace's faith has played a central role in motherhood for her. "I can't separate my children from my spirituality and my faith. They are a gift from God."

I loved the feeling of them moving inside me.

"I loved being pregnant; it was a great experience. I loved the feeling of them moving inside me." She went into labor with her first child 2 weeks early, experiencing back pain, and then throwing up in the middle of the night. "My daughter was in the wrong position so we were going to have a C-section, but I went into labor before that happened." Grace's midwives told her to go to the hospital. "So they gave me something for the pain, to get me through the night so the doctor could come in and do a C-section in the morning. I didn't sleep that night. Finally they were able to take away the pain, but I couldn't sleep because my mind was just going. I couldn't believe it was time that we were actually going to see the baby. We didn't know if it was a boy or a girl. I was just lying awake and thinking about how everything was going to change. We were very excited."

How overwhelmed
I was with everything!

In the morning the doctor performed the C-section. "I didn't get to hold her right away because of the C-section, but they brought her to me. I'll never forget my first view of her, her little pink face and a little yellow hat. That's all I could see was this little face. They put her right next to me. I was just crying. It was beautiful."

"I had her and then we got home and how overwhelmed I was with everything. Nursing was painful, more painful than I thought it would be, and the lack of sleep was so hard. Just the amount of work and also this overwhelming sense of responsibility, like oh my gosh, I'm responsible; I can't send her to the nursery. We're it, we're the parents."

I had this overwhelming wave of love for her,
this deep kind of ache.

"Something nobody ever warned me or told me about was that sometimes it takes a while to attach and to feel that bond with your baby. I thought it would be immediate, but I was so overwhelmed that I wasn't feeling the joy. It was like, where's the joy in this? This is hard. I'll never forget that when it clicked for me, I was about a month into it. I was just holding her and looking at her and I had this overwhelming wave of love for her, this deep kind of ache. That was it. It took a while. I do wish somebody had said that it doesn't always happen that you fall instantly in love. But I did with my other ones. I think because I didn't have all the overwhelming newness of everything. That was very meaningful to me when that clicked in, that feeling, and it has never left. It is different than any other kind of love."

As a new mother, Grace eagerly explored the current literature about mothering and taking care of babies. "I remember I had the book, *What to Expect the First Year*, when we first brought her home. I was looking at that and referencing it and finally I just said, 'forget it.' I felt like it was causing me more stress, like I'm not doing things right, or that type of thing." She quit looking at it and decided, "I know how to do this. I know how to show love. I realized that I was good at it, and had good natural instincts about what they needed."

After she had two daughters, Grace remembers, "I was going through one of those times when I wasn't finding the joy, and struggling in my marriage, although not able to identify that yet, but something just wasn't right. I remember being in church and praying about it and feeling this sadness. I had that experience of God talking in my heart. I was quiet enough to hear, 'Don't worry; everything is going to be okay. It's all going to be okay.'" Shortly after that Grace found out she was pregnant with their third daughter; it was a surprise. "What a great joy she has been. I think that God knew what I needed. There was a time after she was born where I was blissfully happy."

When her children were little, Grace was a stay-at-home mom. "I would go through periods of finding great joy, and things seemed to be going well. And then I would have times where I would go, this is so hard, these days are so long, I need a break. My husband would come home and I would be like, 'I just need a minute.' My kids were good, it wasn't that. It was just that there were times where it wasn't fulfilling. It was a lot of work, and sometimes the same thing day in and day out. They needed so much from me, starting off with changing diapers, feeding them from my body, and then feeding them their meals, everything, that I really didn't think a whole lot about my needs." Sometimes it felt like she was in "survival mode," just trying to get through the day.

I think I could have been a better mother at times had I thought more about my own needs.

"I put a lot on hold, particularly when my children were young. I really didn't think a whole lot about my needs. There was no time for mine. In hindsight, I think I could have been a better mother at times had I thought more about my own needs and did some things for myself that would feed me a little bit. That is something I know now that I am older."

"Socially, I became closer with my sisters. I have two sisters and we all had babies around the same time. In fact, with our last babies we were all pregnant at the same time.

So that became how we connected. We would get together with our little ones. I did the same thing with friends too. I met a couple of women through ECFE (Early Childhood Family Education); one today is still a very good friend of mine. We connected through our children. I relied on those supports for those days when you have little ones and you are just craving an adult conversation. Looking back, I think that got me through the things that were tough because we had each other, and we could talk about the things we were going through. That was a huge part of my life with my little children, was getting together with other moms."

We were the really good parents
but we didn't have an intimacy, a connection.

Motherhood has shaped who Grace is. "It had a huge impact on my identity. I am very much identified as a mother first and foremost above anything else. I would say in one way that wasn't good. I lost my identity as a wife and eventually got divorced. In hindsight, I identified so much as a mom, and only a mom, that I didn't identify enough as a wife and put enough energy into that relationship. I would say my husband was the same way. We were the really good parents but we didn't have an intimacy, a connection. We weren't growing that. Looking back, that wasn't good."

The divorce was a catalyst for much of Grace's personal growth as a woman. "I felt like my life really began after my divorce, for me, and my development as a woman. I am much happier. It is like two separate things for me. I had this life with my young children and then it changed after the divorce. I actually think I became an even better mom because I was having more time to take care of my needs and work on things with me."

Despite the guilt she felt about the divorce, she tried to make things easier for them in all the decisions that she had to make going forward in her life. "When I went back to work again, because of the divorce, I worked for a woman who was very compassionate about my wanting to be with my children, and so I only worked during school hours, and not every day. She honored that I wanted to be home for them still when they came home from school. I am really grateful that I had the luxury of doing that. It was always very important to me to be there for them. Even with the divorce, making sure that even though so many things changed, certain things didn't change for them, and that was one of them. They have always come home after school to me and I wanted that to continue, so every day they did."

Grace felt fortunate that her ex-husband was supportive even through the divorce. "There were many times that I thought how lucky I was. The father of my children is a wonderful father, and the fact that he was willing to have them half the time was so helpful for our girls because they didn't really lose either one of us. They had us as much as they possibly could. How lucky I was to be in that position. I wasn't really single parenting."

There is nothing that my children could ever do
that would make me abandon them,
to ever stop supporting them,
to stop loving them.

Grace's relationships with her parents changed after her divorce. "That is a deep pain in my life. My mom's relationship with my dad was one of subservience, and when I got divorced they disowned me. It was driven by my dad, because that is not the type of person my mom is." Over the years Grace has went back and forth between feeling compassion for her mother and being angry with her. "It was a choice. There are lots of different reasons for why she made it, the world that she lives in, but she still made that choice to disown me, abandon me." It has been 10 years, and by choice her parents no longer have a relationship with their grandchildren either. Grace has learned from this painful experience that although she is similar to her mother in some ways, she also knows that she is very different too. "There is nothing that my children could ever do that would make me abandon them, to ever stop supporting them, to stop loving them."

Grace is remarried. In her new marriage she became a stepmother to five children from her husband's previous marriage. "The idea is that I wanted to treat my stepchildren the same way I treat my children, that they feel loved and cared for. What I found though is that it is really hard for them to accept that sometimes. They have conflicted feelings because they have a mom."

I'm damned if I do,
and damned if I don't.

Before she and her husband got married they saw a therapist about blending their families and got some helpful advice, "The goal is inclusion, not intimacy. If intimacy happens that is great, but it is okay if it doesn't." Occasionally Grace is reminded that she will always have "step" in front of her name, and "that even though what I said or did was completely wonderful and beautiful, it will always be accepted in a different way because I am a stepmother." It can be frustrating and hurtful at times for Grace. "It is that feeling of—I'm damned if I do, and damned if I don't." As a stepmother, Grace continues to make the goal inclusion. "It is a very difficult role. Even when I feel like we have the best situation because the kids get along great, we still have our difficulties."

I think a happier mom
is a better mom
for her children.

"I do believe you become a better mother when you are meeting your needs, whether it is physical or spiritual or whatever. I think a happier mom is a better mom for her children." Grace describes herself as a very happy, balanced, and fulfilled mother. "I'm in a good place and I feel that I'm a good mom." Sometimes her husband comments on what a good mom she is, or her kids will say something to that effect. "It feels really good to hear that because like I said, I always wanted to be a mom and identify with that. It's been my 'job.' You work a regular job and you get reviews and you might get a raise or a bonus, but that doesn't happen at all in the job of motherhood, so I really do appreciate those affirmations whether they are from my husband or my children, when they have written something or say something to me. I really hang on to that."

As her kids get older she has learned that the hugs and kisses do not come as freely: "I made an effort, a mental effort first, because it dawned on me that we weren't hugging and touching. When they are little you touch all the time and I realized when they got older, that we never touch. I'm not an aggressive person but I realized they are adolescents and that it is just not in their minds anymore. I missed it so I made an effort in my mind, I said, 'okay I am going to initiate hugs and things like that." So I have been doing that a lot more now."

I love the whole thing.
I just love being a mom.

When Grace reflected on what she enjoys most about being a mother, she said, "I love the whole thing. I just love being a mom. I just like being together. I appreciate that more because I don't have them with me every day. I just love being with them. I don't really think about it because it is my life and I'm happy and I enjoy it. I like laughing with them, now that they are older. We did a family game night a couple weeks ago and it was really fun. We just laughed a lot. They spend so much time with their friends and wanting to do social things that those times are more rare." Grace loves watching them grow and develop their own interests as well. "My two youngest are dancers and so I love watching them dance. I find a lot of joy in that."

That love that I talked about, and that ache,
it really drives everything.

Grace acknowledges that parenting children through adolescence can be difficult at times. "As the kids got older, the challenge was sometimes their emotional swings and navigating that changing relationship. I felt like I was a very good mom when they were little. It was way easier than being a mother to adolescence, and I long for those days for when their love for me was so unconditional. I was their world and I could do no wrong. Then you become a parent of an adolescent and all of a sudden they are very critical of you." As her children grow closer to becoming adults, Grace still makes her decisions based on what is best for them. "That love that I talked about, and that ache, it really drives everything."

Mothering teenagers and young adults had made Grace aware of the fact that she is a primary role model for them. "I am very aware of setting a good example with eating habits, even my alcohol consumption, modeling moderate behavior and that kind of thing. I would never overindulge in front of them. As far as exercise and that type of thing, I am very active and I have that structured into my life and I hope they notice. I don't say to them directly, 'see what I am doing, it's a good thing for life,' but I would hope that I am modeling for them that it is nice to have balance in your life, and taking care of your body. Also spirituality, and all of those things. There is definitely a part of me that does it for them, as far as setting a good example, with a healthier lifestyle."

Grace has also set professional goals for her own future. "Going back to school was really good for me, seeing that I still do have intelligence, and again the modeling. They don't give a lot of feedback when they are teenagers, but I would hope that on some level they look at what I am doing and think that it is cool and are proud of me. They might not get that now, but maybe when they are older and they are moms and they think about it, they might be like, 'I can't believe mom did that.'"

Tara's Story

The biggest word is hope,
there is hope.
—Tara

"I first became a mom when I was 16. I didn't know what to expect as far as delivering and all of that. The labor was scary at that point. As far back as I can remember I was really feeling like I was being punished because my labor and delivery was so painful, and I was in labor for hours, and hours, and hours. That was really horrible." Tara's first moments of being a mother were difficult. She felt the stigma and shame of being young and pregnant out of wedlock. "I was in a hormonal mood at the time where you are feeling like you don't know who you want to be mad at, and feeling kind of lonely because the father of the baby didn't want to come up to the hospital and see her right away."

Tara gave him an ultimatum: "If you don't come up and see her you are never going to have a relationship with her because you are never going to see her, period. If you are not a father now, you are not going to be one later. So then he came up to the hospital, drunk, and tried to break the emergency room door down. It was an awful experience. It was so embarrassing."

Tara's experiences prior to giving birth to her daughter were also challenging. She had a male doctor who did many more prenatal checks than were necessary, and began telling her things that scared her. "So he said he needed to see me after hours up at the clinic, and that just didn't sit right with me. He had done all these extra clinical visits with me prior to that so I finally told somebody about it and they went after him. He (the doctor) quit his job after that and went somewhere else. As far as doctors go, it was pretty creepy." This led to more fear for Tara, who was already scared about being such a young mom. "That really gave me an uncomfortable feeling about doctors after that. So that wasn't a very good start."

*My mom was an abusive mother
to me growing up.*

Tara did not have a supportive family to help her with the new baby. "My mom was an abusive mother to me growing up. I was the oldest. I had to set a good example. She was physically, emotionally, and verbally abusive to me. So she wasn't for me, and that is why I moved out when I was sixteen. I had to get away from her. I felt so hurt by her, and I didn't want to be there living with my child. She had a baby at that point too, from a different father than mine. I thought one baby in the house was enough, so I decided to move out."

*It's not about you anymore,
its about your child and their needs.*

Tara quickly went from being a teenager in high school living with her mother to being a full-time mother living on her own. "I was very protective of my child at the time when I became a mother. I grew up really, really fast. I didn't feel like I was ever sixteen. I didn't feel like I was ever a kid, or a teenager, because after that I had to get responsible and be there like now. Being a mother means growing up really, really quickly. It is a lot of responsibility. Knowing that it's not about you anymore, it's about your child and their needs."

I remember feeling so inadequate.

Tara felt the stigma of being a young teenage mother in her small rural community. "When you go to church and you are a single mom and you are a young mom, you get looked at like you don't fit in here, you shouldn't be here because you're not married and you don't have the husband and you are not that typical family person. So everybody would give you the look. I remember feeling so inadequate."

Tara moved from an abusive mother to an abusive partner. "The father of my child was abusive. Nothing I ever did was good enough or right. That added complications. No matter what it was about, her feeding or changing or anything, he would negate me or abuse me emotionally about that. That made it very hard. He didn't live with me but he kind of did. He was five years older. He could have been charged with statutory rape but my parents didn't pursue that."

Being a young teenage mother, and living with an abusive man, Tara felt immense pressure to be perfect. "I was this mom who was more worried about how everything looked and appeared than about nurturing and getting close and really caring for my child like I did later on in life with my youngest daughter. I regret that part, being young like that and not being able to understand how important that is. But then my mother was also not that way with me. She didn't nurture me. She wasn't close to me, so I didn't have that closeness and that bonding with her, I don't think ever. That was something I had to really focus on later on in life when I had my third child."

"Becky, my second daughter, came six years later, because of course I didn't want to have a baby out of wedlock, and at such a young age again. So I was going to wait awhile because I had felt so embarrassed by having a child so young, which was not a good thing back then. When I had her, I was married to the abuser by then, and still doing the same perfectionist type things as a mom. I think I bonded with her a little bit better because I was older, and thinking that I have to do something different. She is a funny one; she brought a lot of joy into our lives, well, mine anyway. I don't think you could bring joy to my abuser."

You get them dressed, feed them breakfast,
but you are still thinking in the back of your mind,
what is he going to do to me today?

Those years from Tara's first marriage were some of the most difficult she remembers. "When I was married, I felt really isolated. Motherhood wasn't like going out with other friends that I knew. Most of them were still in high school, and doing something else, so I wasn't there. I was home. My ex-husband wouldn't let me go to high school or let me finish. I felt really by myself, alone, as a mom. Then with my own mom not being close to me, or being nurturing, or having that. I didn't have her help either." Living in an abusive situation made it more difficult for Tara to be a good mother to her two daughters. "You aren't really deeply there for them emotionally or mentally. You get them dressed, feed them breakfast, but you are still thinking in the back of your mind, what is he going to do to me today? What is he going to get mad over? When is the next time he's going to physically abuse me?"

The only reason why I'm even here,
and even want to stay alive
is because of my girls,
because of my kids.

When her middle daughter was about 5, Tara made the decision to leave her abusive husband. "The only reason why I'm even here anymore, and even want to stay alive (because that is the point to where I got, I didn't even want to live anymore), is because of my girls, because of my kids." Being a young mother in an abusive situation caused Tara to become vigilant about shielding her daughters from the reality of what was happening in their home. "My focus was more on them because I tried not to focus on all the other bad stuff, and the abuse that was going on. I was trying to protect them all the time from that. Keeping them safe from it was my goal until I got out of there."

She was my angel.
She really spoke into my life.

Tara got out of her abusive marriage and received help from a women's shelter, where later on she became very involved helping other women escape abusive relationships. "When you work with battered women and they come into shelters, they have a tough time focusing on their children, and what their needs are. I absolutely, totally understand that because it is not easy. You are thinking about, 'Okay, is he going to beat me up so bad that I'm not going to live?

Who is going to take care of my kids? What's going to actually happen next?' The focus is always on him, or the abuse, the violence, the violence, the violence. It's not on the kids. That is the sad part of it."

Tara credits the help she received at the women's shelter as having made a critical difference in her mothering. "The advocate that I had was tremendous, a really good mom. She showed me a lot of things about what good motherhood is, which helped a lot." Tara grew in courage and confidence. "I set some goals. I finished high school, and went on to technical college for cosmetology, and got my license." Speaking of her advocate from the shelter she says, "She was my angel. She is 11 years older than me, a beautiful woman. She is very spiritual. So she would pray with me, things like that. She really spoke into my life. Spoke good, real good into my life, good, and normal, and fresh and loving things, things that taught me how to look more positively at my life and how to expand on that. I don't think you can really do that without having a spiritual component, not as a mom, not as a human being. That is strongly where my motherhood has tremendously gained in ways, and being able to pour that into my twelve-year old all these years. That is the piece that kept me going, the piece that kept me moving forward and knowing there was more good than bad; there was hope. The biggest word is hope, there is hope."

We go horseback riding together.
We bake cookies together.
We read together.

Tara became a mother to her third daughter when she was older, and in a healthier more stable marriage than before. "I think I am a lot more fun now. I have a lot more peace and I care about that relationship with her more than anything. Work is not more important. Anything else doesn't match up to that relationship that I want to have with her. Even though I sometimes find myself kind of drifting away from that, I pull myself back because she needs that, she really needs that so someday she becomes a mom that loves and nurtures and supports her children in every way possible. So we go horseback riding together, we bake cookies together. We read together." Tara has let go of much of the fear and anxiety she had as a young mom. "I like being an older mom. I really do. You think about the more important things as far as motherhood goes, like how much time you are spending with them, where they are at in their lives, especially in the teenage years."

Now that her youngest daughter is a teenager, Tara is cognizant of keeping the lines of communication open, and being present for her daughter. "I try to let her know what is important and what is really going to matter at this point in her life. Just spending time with her and doing things like going horseback riding, things like that. We go for a lot of long walks together, which is fun. She enjoys having me do her hair, highlighting, or braiding, or all that kind of stuff. Her girlfriends like to come over. I'm a second mom most of the time to these other girls. They enjoy coming over and me doing things with them."

She continues to nurture the bonds she has with her daughters. "I enjoy our talks, lots of giggling and laughs. My middle daughter is very funny. Get the three of us together and we are a bunch of goofballs. We have a really good time just talking about grandkids." Tara feels fortunate to live close by her four grandchildren, and sees them regularly. "I love being a grandma. They are so fun."

Tara's spiritual life continues to play a prominent role in what motivates her to keep going and trying to do her best. "I go to a lot of women's faith meetings. Just hearing their stories, their mistakes, they are so open with who they are and what they are, the mistakes they have made, they are not afraid to share them, and also show how God walked them through that, the spiritual part of how they rectified it and moved forward."

I believe the most important thing
you can do for them is be there.

Tara knows that she is an important source of support and encouragement to her daughters. "It means so much to me that now I'm still trying to speak into their lives and tell them what good mothers they are, making sure they feel solid in who they are as a mom." Tara knows firsthand what a difference it makes in the lives of children when their mothers are supportive and truly present. "I believe the most important thing you can do for them is be there for them. Be a mom. I just keep trying to pour that into her. With all my girls, I try showing them what a good mother looks like."

I am transparent; I am human.
I'm going to make mistakes.

Tara has also pushed herself to succeed professionally, wanting her daughters to see not a picture of perfection, but a woman who is going to keep trying. "If you really, really try hard enough and work at it hard enough you can accomplish much. You can have these goals, you can set them, and you can do them. I try to look at all the positives. You can go for that goal. You still might not get it, but that's okay. I cared about her enough to do that, to try to succeed. You are going to have disappointments, and it is still going to be okay. You still have to pick up, and you are going to have to move forward. Things like that show her that I am transparent; I am human. I'm going to make mistakes, and I'm going to say I'm sorry when I'm wrong. You have those little times when you say things you didn't mean to say, or do things you didn't mean to do."

I believe valuing our relationships
might be the most important thing
I ever teach my children.

"For me, I believe valuing our relationships might be the most important thing I ever teach my children, and to be a hard worker. Because if you don't have people, and you don't have those relationships, you don't get very far in life I don't think. Money can't buy you happiness, but if you have people who really care about you and who you really trust, that's good."

The Ninth Sacred Question

Is there a wounded child inside me?

Self-reflection about your childhood requires time and space to safely unfold your feelings and experiences. Contemplate the following questions with words, artwork, letters, music, or whatever way feels best to you. You may want to go through these questions with a trusted friend, coach, or counselor.

Take time, be gentle with yourself, and don't rush the process.

- What are your most painful memories from childhood?
- Why was this so painful for you?
- Did you have unmet needs as a child?
- How did this affect you?
- Do you have emotional triggers from your childhood?
- Are you still angry, sad or resentful?
- Who are you angry or resentful with?

- Are there patterns from your childhood that you are bringing into your family life?

- What have you learned from your childhood experiences?

- How have you become a stronger and wiser person?

- What is the vision you hold for your own family?

- Are you ready to release the past?

- Can you offer forgiveness to those who have hurt you?

- Who and what has been a source of support to you?

- How can you begin healing your life now?

- What are some ways you can re-parent yourself?

Is there a wounded child inside me?

Gabrielle's Story

*I often just think of myself as Gabrielle,
and my son as Noah,
and we are getting through this world together.*
—Gabrielle

G abrielle had her first child, a baby girl, when she was 30. It was a model pregnancy. "I did yoga my whole pregnancy, and I worked until three days before I gave birth." Gabrielle labored at home and arrived at the hospital already dilated to 9 centimeters. "I gave birth an hour and half later and our daughter was born with a 9 on the Apgar scale which meant she was really healthy." There were even medical students in her delivery room watching her birth process because she was doing it naturally without any pain medication or other interventions. "So there was a sort of pride and maybe naiveté about how blessed I was or how perfect the pregnancy was. It was a whirlwind experience."

However, when Gabrielle and her husband went home with their baby girl, tragedy struck. "On our second day at home, she died in her sleep unexpectedly. We called the hospital and called 911 when she wasn't breathing. My husband tried to do CPR on her and it didn't work. She was just 4 days old." It took about 6 months for them to find out what actually happened to their daughter. She had undetected abnormal cells in her heart. "That experience really shaped how my husband and I became parents." Shattered, Gabrielle knew that she would never want to get pregnant again if she didn't do it right away. "We had a bunch of tests done on ourselves and there was nothing wrong so we got pregnant right away, six months after we lost her."

I tried to control the situation
but I think parenting isn't controllable.

Gabrielle's next pregnancy was carefully monitored with extra appointments with her doctor. Her doctor had also been sad and upset about the sudden death of Gabrielle's baby girl. "I was a much different person during that pregnancy. I was super nervous. I was really scared that it was going to repeat itself." Her approach was more cautious this time. "I had a whole birthing plan. I even had four copies of it written up just in case my doctor wasn't going to be there. I tried to control the situation, but I think parenting isn't controllable."

Even as she was still grieving the death of her daughter, she was celebrating the new life growing within her. "The pregnancy was relatively uncomplicated and I had another natural childbirth. I was able to do that powerfully." Her labor was harder this time, but she had done it before and she knew she could do it again. Some things, however, were different for Gabrielle. "We had a lot of specialists in the room. I had to have a monitor the whole time. I was an at-risk pregnancy." Gabrielle, at the age of 32, delivered a healthy baby boy. "We had heart specialists doing a bunch of tests on him immediately after birth. Nothing was wrong."

The loss of the first child
made me a much more careful parent
and probably less relaxed.

Gabrielle noticed that other people were apprehensive as they congratulated her and her husband on their new baby boy. She and her husband approached this birth differently as well. "My husband actually took pictures of the whole birthing process with my daughter, but not so many pictures with my son." Gabrielle felt more wary. "I definitely think that the loss of the first child made me a much more careful parent and probably less relaxed. I didn't feel invincible. I felt less joy around it."

As her son got older, it bothered Gabrielle that he did not know that he had a sister who had died at birth. "When he was 3 years old I finally told him. My husband was against it kind of, he thought it wasn't appropriate or he didn't need to know about that yet, but I needed to be truthful with him. I felt like it impacted our relationship; there was a distance or dishonesty in my parenting of him, without him understanding what I had gone through. The moment I told my son was a really big moment in our relationship. It made me feel more vulnerable to him and it made me feel like he trusted me more. It made me feel like my story was complete with him." Gabrielle and her son sometimes talk about his sister and about how everything happened. "The one thing I think about a lot of times is if she wouldn't have died I wouldn't have gotten pregnant 6 months later and I wouldn't have my son that I have today."

I wasn't prepared for how much time it took
and how much it changed who you are as a person.

Becoming a parent to her son brought some revelations for Gabrielle about motherhood. "I think that I discovered that I didn't know what I was doing necessarily, that I wasn't prepared for how much time it took and how much it changed who you are as a person." Gabrielle found herself in awe of all the mothers and fathers in the world. "I remember repeating to myself several times, 'I cannot believe other people have done this.' I am a perfectly capable, organized woman. I have multi-tasking skills. I cannot believe other people have done this and actually gotten through it. There are people walking around in the world everywhere that have actually raised multiple children successfully with maybe not even half the skill set that I have and it has worked out somehow." She felt overwhelmed with the number of feedings, the number of diaper changes, the 24-hour job that it is being a mother. "I think I was sort of shocked at how much work it was, and how you really can't prepare yourself for it."

Gabrielle experienced some serious challenges with her husband that greatly impacted her experiences of motherhood. "Long story short, he suffered from mental illness, both depression and a variety of substance abuses that I was not aware of. But his struggles started to become obvious when we had a child." Her husband's mental illness meant Gabrielle had to assume all the responsibility in the care of their son. "My need for him to be responsive and present and take on traditional roles—he wasn't capable of doing that. So when I became a mother, it really changed our relationship significantly because I had to basically take everything on, and I really became the guardian of my son Noah.

I spent much of my time
guarding my son
from the realities of his father's struggles.

"I worked full-time, my husband worked sort of part-time. We still had our child in full-time daycare. That was my reality because us having a child in the constructs of being parents and being present 24 hours a day wasn't something my husband was able to live up to. I sometimes think that maybe he knew that he wasn't up for the task but he loved me enough to go through it with me, and I sensed that. I spent much of my time guarding my son from the realities of his father's struggles."

Gabrielle shouldered a heavy burden. "I was a full-time mother and a full-time caregiver to both my son and my husband." Trying to juggle caring for her son with working full time, and also maintaining her husband, Gabrielle did not have any time for herself. "I was just in survival mode." Her priority was taking care of her son and shielding him from her husband's mental illness. "It had gotten to the point where I wasn't leaving my husband and my son home alone together. We would do tons of things as a family but I wasn't leaving my son; I wasn't feeling trusting of my husband that he would be able to be aware enough to be a caregiver."

There was a part of me that stayed with him.
I loved him.
But I knew for a long time that it wasn't okay.

Gabrielle lined up an apartment down the street for her husband and tried to make sure he was getting help for his mental illness. "There was a part of me that stayed with him. I loved him. But I knew for a long time that it wasn't okay, but I stayed with him because I wasn't going to let Noah go stay with him overnight and stuff without me being there. I was struggling with the idea of if we ever were to separate or divorce; how would that work if I couldn't trust him in the home with our child. How would that work?" Sadly, while they were living apart, her husband committed suicide after his mental illness spiraled out of control, something that Gabrielle never thought her husband would do. The experience has been a difficult hurdle to overcome. "It really hardened me I think, but I have a really sweet relationship with my son."

Gabrielle and her son continue to have a very close relationship. "I am present and honest. That is one thing I can give him as a parent." She has had to adjust to her new role as a solo parent and find ways to set boundaries and yet nurture him at the same time. "Right now my biggest struggles are trying to manage a full life while being a parent. It's all the logistics of parenting, working full-time and finding time to grocery shop, wash clothes, doing all those things." Being present for her son and not becoming distracted by all the details of living is important to Gabrielle; being there for him is her priority. "I don't have a lot of other time carved out for my own self-development or even space to wander and figure out what that would mean."

That is the kind of relationship my son and I have,
we do talk that openly,
which I'm proud of.

As a solo parent, Gabrielle feels the responsibility that she carries for everything in their life. She talks openly with her son about his feelings of loss and grief about his father, although he does not yet know that his father committed suicide, but he knows his father suffered from mental illness and did not take care of his body. She struggles to know when to have that difficult conversation with her son about his father's death. He is starting to ask questions. Gabrielle believes he needs to know the truth before he enters puberty so that he can process the news before he is in that stage of development. Being honest with her son is very important to her. "That is the kind of relationship my son and I have, we do talk that openly, which I'm proud of."

In the meantime, Gabrielle made a special photo book for her son about his father. "I made it with the idea that he would have something to hold onto, memories of his father." She has told her son, "Your memories of your father are your own and they don't all need to be perfect, they are still valuable."

The motherhood component for Gabrielle seems to be on autopilot, and now what she worries more about is finding good male relationships for her son. "Now he doesn't have a father. And I think about: How do I ensure that he has that same support that he deserves? He has a good relationship with my dad and my brother, so we nurture those bonds." Gabrielle has reached out to strengthen the connections they have with family and friends, to fill their life with people that care and love them. Even so, she feels the loneliness at times of being a solo mother to a young boy. "I mean one parent can be enough, but there is an identity thing that happens with children when they have two parents to model after, even when they aren't two perfect parents, or even parents that are together. He doesn't have any alternative than me. I am all he has, and he is very aware of that. That is why I am very aware of being present for him."

The biggest guarantee we can do is fill ourselves with tons of friends and family that do love us.

One of the biggest lessons that Gabrielle is trying to teach her son is that there are no guarantees in life. "The biggest guarantee we can do is fill ourselves with tons of friends and family that do love us, and the odds of someone being around to love us and take care of us are pretty good, that is what we can do to move forward. There is no guarantee that everyone in our life is going to be here forever, but the guarantee we have is to try to have as many of those relationships in our life as we can."

Gabrielle's relationship with her son is the most important thing in her life. "I really enjoy my time with him. I enjoy that I have a relationship with him. He is my family, and I think I have finally made that shift as a woman. My parents are my family too, but really my son is my total family, he's my home. That is something I enjoy. We have a friendship. I enjoy watching him learn and I learn from him." Her role as a mother continues to be core to her identity. "Without him I don't know who I would be."

Sometimes you just need someone
to bounce a couple of ideas off of,
that's what my girlfriends and I
have been for each other.

A significant source of support for Gabrielle in motherhood has been her female friends and family. "I have a couple of really good girlfriends that have allowed me to talk to them about the challenges of parenting. As a solo parent, you don't get those moments where you are able to see your child accomplish something or do something funny and have that moment of reflection or validation that a partner provides you with. I don't have that with anyone else so my girlfriends have become that for me. I am able to complain about or even be proud of or just even find something humorous my son does and my friends take the time to provide me that kind of validation and feedback; it is usually just simple things but you need that as a parent. My parents have been very supportive but not in that same way. Sometimes you just need someone to bounce a couple of ideas off of, that's what my girlfriends and I have been for each other."

After her husband's death, Gabrielle's spiritual beliefs have changed. She feels her husband's presence around her all the time, and in her dreams he is very real. "Ever since my husband died I do believe in an afterlife, which I didn't believe in before. That has sort of shook me about my preconceived notions, that religion wasn't necessary. I am just not sure how to engage in the church setting, but I feel my husband here."

Gabrielle was raised in a Christian church, but she and her husband did not practice any religion. Her husband was an atheist, and she had never liked the dogmatic teachings of the church. "I was always the kid in church that raised her hand and asked why we had to obey the rules. I was very argumentative around that, even as a young child. I was always against how women were generally considered second-class citizens in the confines of Christianity." Even though she had not been practicing any form of religion, after having a child she began to explore this area of her life again. "I felt an urge to introduce my son to some form of religion, maybe even a historical and cultural component of it for developmental purposes." Gabrielle has no desire to impose any belief system on her son, and said they are still finding their way.

Life is what you make it,
even when there are difficult times
and challenging situations.

Most importantly, Gabrielle does not worry about labels or titles or making life picture perfect for her son. She has learned that life is what you make it, even when there are difficult times and challenging situations. Commenting on motherhood Gabrielle said, "I don't know if I am always doing it right, and the job doesn't pay very much." "I often just think of myself as Gabrielle, and my son as Noah, and we are getting through this world together."

10

The Tenth Sacred Question

Am I willing to be more open, honest and vulnerable?

Contemplate the following questions:

- When it comes to your children, what do you fear most?

  Example: That I will not always be there to protect them and keep them safe.

- What overwhelms you?

  Example: The piles of dishes, mounds of laundry, and messy house. I just don't have time to keep up with everything.

- Do you feel a sense of separation from your children? Why?

  Example: When life gets busy and we don't have time to connect or laugh, or snuggle and just be together.

- Is there something you have been waiting to share with your children? What's holding you back?

  Example: I've never told my children about (fill in the blank), I'm afraid it would disappoint or disturb them too much.

- Do you ever feel inadequate? Why?

  Example: I see other mothers who seem to have it all together, meanwhile, I'm falling apart inside.

  Are you holding yourself to an impossible ideal, trying to be "the perfect mother"? How does it feel?

  Example: I am constantly comparing myself to other moms. I would like to have more self-compassion and self-confidence as a mother.

Am I willing to be more open, honest and vulnerable?

Alexandra's Story

Everyone says I must be so strong,
but I had to be smiling for my children...
I had to live and be there for them.
—Alexandra

A lexandra was living at home with her parents in Russia and going to college when she became pregnant with her first child. "I had my first child when I was 18. For a Russian woman having her first baby between the ages of 18–26 is considered healthy and ideal. I had wanted to be a mom since I was a child." Alexandra was surprised and yet very excited to have a baby. "I was very happy when I got pregnant knowing I wanted a child. Can I say that I was consciously making a child or working on it? No, but I think subconsciously I was predisposed to be a young mom naturally because I wanted it. To go into the details of how it happened—I just didn't know how to use birth control." Alexandra married the father of her baby while she was pregnant, but soon afterwards he had to leave for the army, which in Russia is a 2-year obligatory service for young men. Alexandra continued living with her parents in their tiny apartment while her husband was away.

She was so beautiful and calm
—a very happy baby.

Alexandra's main focus in life as a new mother was taking care of her infant daughter and being a good student. "I was going to be a young mom and I was going to be responsible." Alexandra discovered that she had a strong mothering instinct. She stayed at home with her family where she had help with her baby girl. "She was a very easy baby. She slept well. She was so beautiful and calm—a very happy baby. She loved nursing, would never take a pacifier or a bottle, and loved touching my ears when she was about to fall asleep. I was a full time student at the time. My mom was helping me in the afternoon when I was at school. Mornings were full of little tasks, like taking a stroll with Sasha outside in any weather, rinsing the little rags that were used instead of diapers (those were still to come to Russia), and nursing. For two years I was with my parents and they helped me."

Having her parents support during those first 2 years of her daughter's life made it easier for Alexandra to go to school and still have a close bond with her child. "I nursed for a year and a half while I was a full-time student. My college was a five-minute walk from my parents and that helped. I knew that I had to get good grades in college, as I was responsible and wanted to be a good provider for Sasha."

Alexandra's husband came back for the birth of their daughter. "He just came once when I gave birth and left again for a year. So we grew apart naturally and when he came back he was a stranger." They divorced shortly after he came back from the army. Alexandra decided to rent her own apartment after getting divorced from her husband. "That was the beginning of the hardships in my life. I was very busy with raising her and studying. I finished college with Master's in English and German Education with straight A's and a GPA of 4.0."

I was by myself,
a single mom.

Alexandra signed her daughter up for daycare once she turned 2 years old. "In Russia we had a centralized free public daycare system. It started at the age of sometimes 1, mostly 2, when kids can hold a spoon." "The last two years of college were rough because of the daycare, she would catch colds and I wouldn't have anyone close to me to help. It was an hour and a half bus ride away from my parents. It was close but we had to take a bus because I didn't have a car. It would take forever, two buses, with all the stops. It was horrible. Those two years were rough. I was by myself, a single mom."

Alexandra still spent as much time as she could with her family, on weekends and summer breaks, but her mother had developed severe rheumatoid arthritis and could not help Alexandra take care of her daughter as much. "My daughter had grandparents that she saw every weekend that loved and adored her. She had her own mom (me) with her always and she knew that no matter what happens in my relationships, that I love her. In the summer we were at the cabin all together. It was a beautiful place in a very nice nature preserve. My grandma left it to us as an inheritance, the cabin. We were surrounded with nature." This place in Russia has always been very special to Alexandra's family, who are atheistic in their beliefs, but worship nature as their form of spirituality.

After Alexandra finished college she got a job and began teaching English while her daughter went to daycare, where she continued to get sick. "Sasha had chicken pox and it hit her immune system. For four years in a row, like two months every year she would be in the hospital with kidney infections, (hospitals were free). Then it came to a point where she started having her gut flora killed by antibiotics, and she started having all kinds of other issues." Alexandra herself also experienced some health problems with her pancreas and inflammation. "I didn't know how to take good care of myself as far as nutrition, stress management, and rest at the time."

Everywhere money was needed
for the rent,
or clothes, and food.

During this time of "pure survival" Alexandra did everything she could, including taking on extra work as a tutor nights and weekends to provide for herself and her daughter. "I was trying to make extra cash through the tutoring, but to have a permanent flow of students I couldn't raise my prices much, so it was cheap. I had to work many more hours to have a certain amount every month. It was hard. My mom was almost standing on her knees begging me to stop working this hard and I couldn't because everywhere money was needed for the rent, or clothes, and food. In Russia minus twenty can happen three months in a row and you wait for a bus at the bus stop for forty minutes. You get frozen, literally. So you need furry boots, you need furry coats, furry hats, otherwise you can't survive in the freezing cold."

Russia was undergoing massive political changes as Putin came to power and the economic situation was terrible for most people, even those who were educated and employed. Even trying to buy food was an arduous task for Alexandra. "Transportation didn't work very well. I ended up waiting for the bus with Sasha, who was bundled up, to get to the store where they sold vegetables. It would take two bus stops and then you would take that in the cold and with a child. That was impossible so we were not eating vegetables. I don't remember what we were eating. I just know it wasn't good for me, or Sasha."

I wanted her to have a guardian angel,
who would protect her.

Alexandra was overworked and hardly sleeping and started experiencing what she calls "demonic encounters." "So I went to church and got baptized, and I would have a cross on me and I would say the Lord's Prayer, and any visions or encounters went away immediately. I also baptized Sasha. I wanted her to have a guardian angel, who would protect her." Alexandra became interested in spirituality. "I needed something that would guide my life, something light and powerful that would help me."

One day during this difficult period of her life Alexandra was waiting at the bus stop with her daughter crying and feeling lost, not knowing what to do about her daughter's health problems. Her daughter had again been put on antibiotics for an infection and the antibiotics were not helping anymore. A woman at the bus stop came over and told Alexandra she knew a healer who could help her daughter. "She introduced me to one of the most powerful psychics who worked with just the power of his thinking. Sasha had 100,000 white blood cells in her blood in one week without touching her, from just a few sessions." Alexandra and her daughter both experienced miraculous healings, which began Alexandra's subsequent interest in health and healing. "He introduced me to a group of people who were doing meditation, healing. There were Reiki healers among them, and that is how I began, and now I am a Reiki master."

She kept asking me for a daddy.

It became clear to Alexandra that her daughter missed having a father in her life. "She kept asking me for a daddy. She would say, 'Mom, go find one, I need a Dad.' She would cry. You know it is a serious case when the child knew she needed a dad and was asking for one."

However, the prospects in Russia at that time were not good for Alexandra. "In Russia guys drink, smoke, change mistresses, and in my city there were seven women for one man. They go naked in front of guys; they jump in Jeeps and do all kinds of things just to find their prince. The pressure of getting dressed up and using make-up is so high that people go take garbage out and buy bread at the grocery store next door dressed in high heels and bright red lipstick, because what if Prince Charming happens to be there? What if somebody sees you looking plain?"

Alexandra was also experiencing a lot of sexual harassment, a common occurrence for women in Russia, and she hated it. "It was happening a lot. You cannot even walk along the street, a car would come, and someone would offer you to go somewhere. A lot of girls would give themselves for a bottle of beer, again hoping that love happens. It was bad."

Someone came for me
like Cinderella...

Alexandra decided to put her profile on the Internet in the hopes of finding someone outside of Russia. "My wish was to finally get married and get settled and for Sasha to have a dad." Alexandra soon met an American man over the Internet who lived in Alaska. "He came and visited me once and was very different from the Russian guys. He didn't have that burden of stress or worry. He had big blue eyes and looked like a body lifter, and very naïve and very kind. He was super nice to my daughter and it won my heart, yes, right away, that someone came for me like Cinderella, from the USA."

Soon after, Alexandra and her daughter moved from Russia to Fairbanks, Alaska in the middle of winter to join her new husband and his daughter, who lived with him in the summertime. Alexandra remembers her new home in Alaska as a place where there was no sun; it felt to her like a dying Russian countryside village. "I was naïve, but that naiveté helped me. I was still happy with everything, meditating, saying prayers, thanking him for what I have and that I have a husband. Sasha has a dad. It was a nice peaceful life. I was a very good wife."

Alexandra's daughter was 4 years older than her husband's daughter, and the two girls soon became friends. "They were really good sisters to each other and I would watch them play while he was working in the summer." Alexandra secured a job teaching English during the school year and made friends with other women in the community. "I met a very cute sweet Russian girl right away when we came. She got me to know other Russian women, and she was my light, there was light from her. And we helped each other a lot. We were friends with families. Sasha was best friends with her daughter, so that was beautiful. I was helping a lot of Russian women with driving, and English. I felt needed with Reiki. I was giving Reiki classes actively. I was happy."

I can't have just one child,
it's impossible.
I needed two at least.

During this time Alexandra tried to convince her husband to have a child with her. "Something inside of me said 'I can't have just one child, it's impossible. I needed two at least.' But he wouldn't reverse his vasectomy. He had his child." Eventually Alexandra and her husband decided to move to the Midwest where his daughter lived during the school year so he could see her more. "We slept on the floor at his mom's for a year and a half. We didn't have a room or a bed, and Sasha was being tormented by his mom. She wasn't nice to Sasha, but I was thankful we had shelter, and good relationships. I told Sasha to be patient; someday she would be an adult."

After finding jobs Alexandra and her husband were able to buy their own house. "It was a nice home and next to nature and farms. She had good friends. She was able to go to a horse farm and learn how to take care of horses." Alexandra's daughter remembers it as "the happiest time of her life." However, soon after, Alexandra's marriage fell apart and she decided to leave her husband.

I was in love...
that was when my dream
of having more children came true.

After her divorce, Alexandra fell in love with a Russian man who was teaching her Spanish. "We moved in with him. I was in love, and that was when my dream of having more children came true. We prayed, we invited the soul, and we were married." Alexandra's daughter was a teenager by now and wanted a sister. "We got pregnant. He had a job at that time and I took a leave of absence." They had a healthy baby girl and Alexandra was overjoyed to have another child.

Two years later, Alexandra became pregnant again. While she was pregnant, her husband, who did not have permanent citizenship in the United States, had to go back to Russia to get a new visa to continue working in the United States. "All of a sudden, he had to leave the country immediately. So I was pregnant again, with no place to stay, and he had to leave the country. I am under the blue sky, pregnant, and I have 2 children to care for."

I am happy he's not here
because if the guy could leave his children…
then let him go.

Alexandra gave birth to another daughter on her own, and soon came to the realization that her husband was not coming back from Russia. "I was going to have to raise the children by myself. He left and met somebody in Russia. I am happy he's not here because if the guy could leave his children like that, then let him go." Throughout this difficult time in Alexandra's life, she continued to put the needs of her children first. "My daughter lost her mind over her dad moving and she was depressed. So I was trying to distract her with gymnastics, and whatever I could." "Everyone says I must be so strong, but I had to be smiling for my children. If we are serious or stone-faced, they will be the same way. So I had to be happy. I had to live and be there for them, take care of them." Alexandra definitely felt older and wiser as a mother by this time.

Reflecting on what it was like to be a teenage mom versus having a baby when she was older, Alexandra is able to see positive and negative aspects in both experiences. About being a young teenage mom, Alexandra said, "You take things easier and your body can handle the challenges. You are stronger and more optimistic about everything, but you are stupid and dumb and ignorant when it comes to raising a healthy child in a healthy home in healthy relationships. I was trying to create it all, and was doing it to the best of my knowledge, but I didn't know much." When Alexandra had her youngest two daughters she was in her 30s, and felt she was better equipped to handle the challenges of raising children. "That is why being older and wiser and knowing things helps to raise healthy children, but it doesn't help your own sanity. You have to be more responsible and you are harder on yourself when you are older."

It was so important to Alexandra to have time with her new baby after she was born that even though she had no husband or job anymore, she still found ways to survive and stay home for an extended leave of absence. When her daughter was about a year old, Alexandra returned to her job teaching English, and picked up the pieces of her life. With encouragement from her friends, she decided to date again, and met the man she is married to now. "He is such a decent person. Amazingly kind, spiritual, loving and very well grounded. He is a real gentleman. When I was with this guy I knew my kids would be happy." When Alexandra first met her husband and introduced him to one of her young daughters, her daughter said, "thank you for finding such a wonderful dad for me." Today, Alexandra has the family that she has always wanted. She has a close relationship with her oldest daughter, who is 22 years old, and pursuing a career as an artist. The two of them go shopping and chat about "adult stuff" now. Special times such as these with her daughter are "such a compensation for all the hardships and challenges that have happened."

I'm in heaven
when I see them happy.

Alexandra describes herself as still being "super responsible" about her children, and continues to learn about health, wellness, and healing. "I feel responsible for what I put in my kids. It is either making them healthy and happy or killing them, it all starts with me." Alexandra acknowledges that it takes a lot of money, time, and energy to raise children, especially buying organic food and supplements, and paying for extracurricular activities, but considers it all worthwhile. "When I see a healthy child smiling and dancing and singing. I'm in heaven when I see them happy." Providing good nutrition for her children is part of being a good mother for Alexandra, and even after working all day she goes home to make "family dinners made from scratch, healthy with vegetables." "I discovered that I find myself looking for ways to stay healthy including my own health as a mom. I am doing my best to make them happy. I do whatever I can do for them to stay healthy and smiling, also having good positive environments to grow in—it is all in the mix. I love being a mother."

After all that Alexandra has been through, it is in the simple and quiet moments with her children that she finds her greatest pleasure. "Little whispers in my ear, 'Mommy, I love you' makes me cry from happiness."

Emilia's Story

Always praise your kids,
tell them 'I love you,'
hug them, and listen.
—Emilia

Emilia became a mother when she was 18 years old. "It was August 12th; that is when I first became a mother. I knew I was pregnant but it was like the whole experience was not what I had ever imagined. The pain and everything. It was wonderful though. I can't explain it. It was just wonderful." Emilia had to drop out of high school after she became pregnant, but she enrolled in adult GED (General Education Development) classes right away. "I had to call the school one day from home and tell them I wasn't coming because I was having labor pains."

Despite her pregnancy being unplanned, Emilia welcomed motherhood. "At that moment when you become a mom, you are not ready for it, but you start caring for that person, that little person that is there with you. There are so many emotions that come with it; it's a wonderful thing." Looking back, Emilia reflected on how being so young when she became a mother affected her own development. "When you become a mom in some ways you grow along with your kids, especially as a teen mom."

After I met my husband
and got pregnant,
everything changed.

There are some things that Emilia wished she could have done differently if she had not become pregnant as a teenager. "I wish I had finished at the high school versus my GED but I guess at that time I wasn't thinking. I still finished, one way or another. I did it." Becoming a mother meant Emilia's plans for the future were no longer possible. "In high school, I had joined the Junior ROTC. I had plans to go into the army, but after I met my husband and got pregnant, everything changed. The army was out of the picture."

Emilia started working at a turkey processing plant and her mother-in-law cared for her new baby daughter. Unfortunately, Emilia had a car accident and sustained injuries that prevented her from working for a while. "After Krista was 3 years old I got pregnant again and then I had a miscarriage. So I had four pregnancies and three babies." Emilia recovered from her injuries and went back to work, this time at a grocery store.

She went from breastfeeding
to a sippy cup right away.

Emilia's second child was another daughter. "I worked for a while when I was pregnant with her, and then I stayed home because I was having some trouble from my car accident, my sciatic nerve had gotten really pinched. After that I stayed home until she was born. I waited like three months and then went back to work." This time she found factory work. Emilia then became pregnant again. "Right after I got pregnant with my third baby, I was working at a factory and I worked my whole pregnancy right until I had her. I got up to go to work and I started having contractions so I didn't go to work. I called and told them I wasn't coming in. Once that happened I went to the hospital and had her. After a while I tried going back to work and I did for the first month, but it was really hard because she wouldn't drink from a bottle, she was only breast-fed so she didn't know how to drink from a bottle. We got through it. She went from breastfeeding to a sippy cup right away because she wouldn't drink from a bottle."

I was pretty much a single mom
with three kids.

By this time Emilia was feeling like a single mom. "My husband was always gone, out of town, or out of state, because he was working construction. So he was gone pretty much all the time. He would come home on Fridays and spend Saturday and Sunday. So on the weekend they had mom and dad, but during the week I was mom and dad. I was pretty much a single mom with three kids. Hard. It was really hard with three."

Between working, taking care of three small children by herself, and running a household, Emilia had a heavy burden at a young age. "It's like you become supermom. You have to because you have to do so many things. You don't think you are capable or able to do all that. You have to be strong. I guess you discover more strength in your person. You are parenting, managing a house, working, and at a young age paying bills, paying rent, everything, taking care of a baby, taking care of a husband. It's so overwhelming. You have to find a way. You have to manage your time. It's like an energizer bunny going and going and going and going, and then you are exhausted." Physically, Emilia tries to take care of herself but admits, "I earned my tiger stripes. I just try to be healthy. The extra pounds that I gained with them; it doesn't bother me that much."

When her girls were little Emilia had some help from her mother-in-law for a few years. "She took Krista and that worked for me, and it worked for her." However, her mother-in-law eventually moved back to Texas where she was originally from. Emilia's family, migrant workers who lived in Texas and worked the peanut and tobacco fields in North Carolina and the beet fields in Minnesota, had left Minnesota to go back to Texas even before her mother-in-law had. However, Emilia chose to stay in the Midwest with her new husband, who was employed at the time. They settled down to raise a family.

> *When I became a mom*
> *it was my baby*
> *and I had to care for her.*

Growing up in a migrant family meant that Emilia was no stranger to children or the reality of caring for them. Emilia watched her mother, a strong woman, work very hard to take care of her seven children while her husband worked in the fields. "Mom carried the load, and Dad was always working." Emilia had been around babies most of her life and felt comfortable taking care of them, but becoming a mother still felt like a new experience for her. "It was a big change for me because now it was my own. Since I am the oldest of seven, I had to take care of my younger siblings, so I was always like a mom. Every day I was caring for everything, not providing financially, but after I started working I did help my parents out a lot. Just being there to help take care of the younger ones. When I came to my own children its totally different. I was responsible for my siblings, but when I became a mom it was *my* baby and I had to care for her."

After her family and her mother-in-law moved away, Emilia had to find someone else to care for her children. She had started working with a migrant school program as a bilingual paraprofessional. "I took the girls to daycare, there was an old lady and they called her grandma. She took care of them for a long time." Eventually Emilia and her husband bought a house in a little town in the area they were living. "At first I wasn't sure, we were out in the middle of nowhere, but now I just love it. I wouldn't move back anywhere else. I love that small town. It is so nice and peaceful and so comforting. The girls love it too. And it's safe. The kids can be out. There are always crazy people everywhere, but it does feel safe for the kids."

I try to be there for my kids
as much as I can.

When describing herself as a mother, Emilia said, "I try to be patient and caring. I try to be there for my kids as much as I can and provide for them the best I can—you know food, clothes. Sometimes it's hard." Reflecting back on her experiences in childhood, Emilia thinks of how she is like her own mother. "My mom is a very caring person. She was always there. I remember things pretty well. She always provided clothing and shelter and everything. She never had time with each and every one of us as individuals because there were seven of us. It was very hard, and I understand that now since I'm a mom and I have three. Sometimes it is like you are so busy with one of them that you can't be with the other two." She described it as, "trying to split myself into three." Although it can be difficult at times, with all the activities that her daughters are in, Emilia stays involved in their lives. Emilia's mother, however, was limited by her circumstances. "My mom didn't have anything at the time for a way to get there because we only had one car when I was growing up, and my dad took it to work. So I am different than my mom in just being able to be there for my kids, like parent conferences and concerts."

Emilia eventually separated from her husband and they have been apart for many years. She described one of her biggest challenges as, "trying to raise my kids on my own and being a single parent." Although it has been difficult, Emilia's intense devotion and sense of responsibility as a mother has meant that she wakes up every morning and does whatever she needs to do to take care of her children. "You have to take it step by step."

We're pretty much always together.

As a single mom, Emilia spends most of her time with her daughters, and enjoys it this way. "I don't know what to do with myself. Okay, what do I do, where do I go? It is like I am lost without them. We're pretty much always together. Since I work at the school, they ride to and from school with me. They will sometimes stop by the office and visit a little bit and then they leave. I can't get away from them (laughter). It's nice."

Emilia continues to have close relationships with her daughters as they get older. "It seems like we are all sisters. We play and joke around. Of course I'm the mom, but yeah, we just do silly stuff and have a sister-type of bond. Yet I'm also strict and crabby sometimes and all of that from being the mom." Emilia's oldest daughter is now 20 and lives with her fiancé. "My oldest daughter lives a block away from us. In the summer she walked from her house to my house, and I walked from my house to her house. She is very close by. When she moved out I missed her but she called me every day, and I would call her. We still call each other. Eventually I got used to it. It's hard."

Reflecting on what or who has been supportive to her as a mother, Emilia got tears in her eyes. Although she has needed help at different times over the years, she has always been hesitant to reach out. "I know there are people out there who are willing to help me but sometimes I don't ask for help. I try to do it all on my own. I try to be a strong parent. I know I have been a strong person but sometimes I think I just take on too much."

Emotionally I'm a crybaby.

Emilia acknowledged that sometimes she feels overwhelmed by the demands that come along with raising three children. "Emotionally I'm a crybaby. There are times when I have to lay down and put a pillow over my head and yell or cry. It's been a learning experience over the years. It's always different. When you have more than one child then it's totally different with each of them."

Emilia feels very fortunate that her three daughters are all doing well in school and in their lives as they grow into young women. "I have good kids." When asked what she would tell other mothers about how to be a good mom, she said, "always praise your kids, tell them 'I love you,' hug them, and listen."

This is what I love about being a mother...

Playing peek-a-boo, tickling his toes, kissing his soft cheeks.

The love I have for my baby is unlike anything—it blows me away.

Maxie, age 22, mother of 1 infant son

Holding her close, feeling her heart beat against mine. I'm in this little bubble where it's just me and her.

Sophie, age 24, mother of 1 infant daughter

The sweet little coos and sighs he makes. Even his hiccups are cute.

Kate, age 25, mother of 1 infant son

It's amazing to me how it feels like I've known her my whole life, yet really we've just met.

I can watch her for hours and everything she does is just so special.

You don't realize how much your own mother loves you until you become a mother yourself.

Miranda, age 26, mother of 1 infant daughter

I love her smiles, and how she looks at me.

I love how she relies on me and that I can be her everything.

I love knowing her dad and I created her, and that through our love, and by the grace of God, we are blessed to have her in our lives.

Brooke, age 26, mother of 1 infant daughter

My mothering instincts—when I became a mother, this part of me came alive that I didn't know was there. Now it's just who I am.

Maria, age 29, mother of 1 daughter & 1 son

The hugs! When my son was a baby, everyone spoke of the smiles, giggles and squirms that I would love and be so proud of... And I was! But the toddler years bring hugs and love like you never thought possible. Even on the worst days, one of those hugs can bring so much peace to a mom.

Kelly, age 31, mother of 1 son

The bond with my son, physically, emotionally, spiritually. As a stay-at-home mom I get a lot of time to really cherish the moments and milestones. I'm building a foundation, a connection for a lifetime with him.

Greta, age 31, mother of 1 son

I love watching him learn and grow. There is something new every day.

I love spending time together and the emotional connection we have.

When I walk in the door, he gets excited and puts his arms out and wants me.

To be loved and needed is so rewarding, so fulfilling.

Erin, age 31, mother of 1 son

Snuggles. I'm fortunate to have a baby that loves to snuggle.

She is always excited to see me. It brings the positivity to life. Cause laundry and bills never smile back at you.

Even when she's teething, my baby is smiling.

Michelle, age 31, mother of 1 infant daughter

Hugs, kisses and snuggles!

Linda, age 32, mother of 1 son & twin daughters

I love everything about it. I can't imagine life without him.

Snuggling with my son. Sometimes he sleeps with us.

I love it when I make him laugh.

Watching him discover something new for the first time.

One of the things I love the most is watching my husband with our baby—to witness their special connection and bond.

Andrea, age 32, mother of 1 son

How fiercely I love my kids, and they love me back.

Katie, age 36, mother of 3 sons & 1 daughter

I love the day-to-day routine of our lives, and the learning and teaching we do for each other.

Mindy, age 36, mother of 2

My kids are 10 and 13 now, so I love how much we can do together. The older they get the more friendship we have.

Trisha, age 37, mother of 1 daughter & 1 son

My children bring me joy everyday. It is different from that of my friends and family—it is so fulfilling and pure.

Consolata, age 37, mother of 2 daughters & 2 sons

I love spontaneous dance parties, late-night bedtime chats, freedom to play and be silly.

The strong visceral connection I have to another human being.

The soft gentle rhythm of breath as she sleeps, brushing her hair, teaching her what it means to be a feminist.

I have increased compassion and empathy for myself and other mamas.

Offering my daughter the gifts of unconditional acceptance, significance, and belonging so she can learn to offer those things to herself.

Amy, age 39, mother of 1 daughter

Watching my children grow into kind, respectful & successful people, knowing I helped influence that.

Desiree, age 40, mother of 2 sons & 1 daughter

It always warms my heart when I ponder how, apart from God who created them, no one in the whole world knows my children better than I do.

My favorite time of day remains at bedtime, when I share snuggles, books, and prayers with my children. There's no better way to end each day!

Kristi, age 40, mother of 2 sons & 1 daughter

I am constantly learning, more about myself really—understanding my limits, what I'm capable of, what my strengths and weaknesses are.

Jessie, age 40, mother of 1 daughter

Belly laughing with my children.

Tina, age 40, mother of 1 daughter & 1 son

The laughter, the fun, they're just silly.

Angel, age 43, mother of 2 daughters, & 1 son

Receiving unconditional love.

Jess, age 44, mother of 2 sons

I love the small, simple, sweet moments motherhood brings. The unexpected...the unplanned...the unrehearsed...and the greatest amount of love that I could have ever imagined...ever!

Amy, age 44, mother of 1 daughter & 1 son

The chance to play, be adventurous, and enjoy fun things together like swimming, skiing, and going to the library.

They teach me so much. They make me laugh. Their fabulous imaginations ignite mine, reminding me to play, stretch, pretend, and consider "what if?"

I'm always grateful for my children. Thank you God. They have made me more than I ever could have been without them, in every single way.

Jenna, age 46, mother of 2 daughters

Being able to be a part of this amazing adventure that my kids go through in the different stages of their lives, and experiencing the joys and sorrows with them.

Bree, age 48, mother of 1 son & 1 daughter

I love snuggling and reading books together.

It's fun to watch how each one is unique.

Robin, age 49, mother of 3 daughters & 1 son

I like my kids. I like who they are. I like watching them grow into who they are going to be, and I enjoy being around them.

Theo, age 50, mother of 2 sons

Knowing that I have changed the world by working with the universe to bring forth these four spirits.

Lisa, age 50, mother of 4 daughters

I love how parenting changes over the span of time, and I like being part of a team with my husband.

Lucy, age 51, mother of 5 daughters

They are just so damn cute. God made kids cute so they would survive.

I love looking at pictures of my kids from when they were little and seeing their happy faces, their goofy grins, and remembering those moments we had together.

Knowing and appreciating how each kid is unique and seeing their special qualities that are different from everyone else.

Having the best conversations with my kids when we're driving together, especially on long road trips.

Jane, age 51, mother of 2 sons and 1 daughter

Being a part of their adult lives. Seeing their interests, how they've grown and who they become. To still be involved gives me a sense of pride, accomplishment, and peace.

Jackie, age 52, mother of 2 daughters & 2 sons

Being a mother has opened so many doors of friendship for me; it's like a built-in social network.

Being a mother gives me purpose every day. It answers the questions: Why am I here? What am I do to with my life?

If I do nothing else but raise four healthy, well-adjusted people that go into this world and make a difference-that will be enough for me. I will feel accomplished and be happy.

Genny, age 53, mother of 4 daughters

At first it was pure awe, selfless love and devotion to each child.

Next, it was enjoying each stage of growth and change, seeing likenesses and both of us in each child.

Now, it is enjoying our adult children, savoring family time and building lasting memories.

Chari, age 57, mother of 2 daughters & 1 son

Watching my kids grow into people who are doing what they are supposed to do, being responsible adults, having good relationships with others, including me.

I can't make them happy, but hopefully I've helped them find the tools they need to make their own happiness.

Kim, age 57, mother of 2 daughters & 1 son

I really liked being a mother because it gave me a purpose. I was important, loved, and needed.

Jody, age 58, mother of 1 daughter & 1 son

The unconditional love that naturally comes out of your heart for your children.

Annie, age 60, mother of 1 daughter & 3 sons

Bringing a new life into the world.

The first flutters in my womb.

Having someone totally dependent on you.

The unconditional love you feel for your child.

It's amazing to watch them grow from a totally helpless baby to a mature and independent adult—knowing I had a part in that.

Ann, age 61, mother of 4 sons

How powerful I feel to be able to conceive, carry, birth, nurse, and nurture a child. My body just naturally knew how to do all that.

Theresa, age 63, mother of 4 sons

Knowing there is always someone there for me. Our relationship is forever. My son is a part of me that will be carried on long after I'm gone.

Elaine, age 63, mother of 1 son

The fun, companionship, and laughter. I'm always learning something new. It's exciting.

I love just being together and sharing our lives.

Sharon, age 65, mother of 1 daughter

I loved it when they were my little babies, it was so easy and simple back then.

Laurie, age 65, mother of 2 sons

That my daughters still need me, and it is mutual. We depend on each other for love and support.

Sally, age 67, mother of 2 daughters

It's my most important purpose in life.

I just loved the breastfeeding, the warmth and connection.

The discovery of each child's personality, and encouraging them with their individual gifts and callings.

Marilyn, age 68, mother of 3 daughters & 1 son

I rocked my babies to sleep. I sung to them. I read them stories every night at bedtime. I'm grateful that I got to do that with my grandchildren too.

I loved watching my kids grow. I liked them in all their stages.

Now, as a grandparent, I can love them up and give them back.

Sandy, age 70, mother of 1 son & 1 daughter

I enjoy watching my children parenting. They are instilling strong beliefs. They are kind, interested in all races, creeds, and religions, and so are their children. I am very proud of all of them.

Mary, age 71, mother of 1 daughter & 2 sons

I love being a mom. My kids are so precious to me. Even though they are all grown up, they are still my babies.

I lost my husband to cancer about a year ago. My kids and grandkids have been so wonderful. They have given me so much comfort.

Shari, age 72, mother of 1 son & 1 daughter

I love the idea that I was able to give birth to 4 good people who are making a difference in the world.

It's good to feel needed, and to have been able to be a part of the development of humanity—plus it was fun!

Judy, age 75, mother of 4 sons

The most important part of my life is my family. My children are my greatest accomplishment.

I always told my girls, "I love you and I like you." And I still do.

The highlight of my day was going home after work and spending time with my children.

Jackie, age 82, mother of 2 daughters

I must have done something right because most of my kids live close by and they come visit me often. My oldest son is retired now and we play cards together every day. They take good care of me.

Arlene, age 84, mother of 7 sons & 1 daughter

We raised our children to be kind people. I have boys that are tender and thoughtful and I love seeing that.

Dottie, age 88, mother of 2 sons

I loved cooking big meals like roast beef, mashed potatoes, and gravy for my family. And we always had to have apple pie. I baked bread, rolls, and cookies. I loved seeing how much they enjoyed it all.

Lu, age 91, mother of 5 daughters & 1 son

I had something good to give in this life—loving my children. And I appreciate all the love I receive back from my children and grandchildren.

Nadine, age 93, mother of 2 daughters

This is an old song by Doris Day that my grandma always sang to me (J.G.):

I love you a bushel and a peck
A bushel and a peck and a hug around the neck
It beats me all to heck, how I'll never tend the farm
Never tend the farm when I wanna keep my arm
About you, about you
'Cause I love you a bushel and a peck
You bet your purdy neck I do
A doodle oodle ooh doo
A doodle oodle oodle ooh doo

In memory of Grandma Bobbie, age 95,
mother of 6 daughters & 3 sons

This is what I find most challenging about motherhood...

Getting enough sleep. Some days I feel like a zombie.

Bella, age 21, mother of 1 infant son

I'm a single mom, working, and in school full-time. I want to make a better life for my daughter, to give her everything she needs. It's difficult, but I'm doing it.

Sophie, age 24, mother of 1 infant daughter

My daughter was born with torticollis (tight neck muscles) and has mild hearing loss. She had to have a lot of physical therapy and wore a helmet for a flat spot on her head. It's fun seeing her make progress and get to a good place now.

Teaching manners...please, thank you, yes and no. You get the cuddles, but you also have to be a parent and help them become the best version of themselves.

Abby, age 25, mother of 1 daughter

Sleep deprivation...it gets better eventually. But I'm pregnant with my second now and I'm not looking forward to going through that again.

Miranda, age 26, mother of 1 infant daughter

I think it is the unknown. Not knowing what my baby needs, the when, and how much, and if she is hungry or tired. I'm starting to know her different tones of cries. I am always worried that something could happen.

I'm always comparing, especially to my sister and how she does things. I know there is more than one way to do things right; it's what works best for you and your family.

I have huge "mom guilt" about working full-time and sending my daughter to daycare. I'm putting so much trust in this one person, giving my pride and joy to someone that I just met. So I'm learning how to be okay with my daughter being at daycare.

I had a rough delivery. I got sad about how everything happened because things did not go as I had planned. Looking back, it doesn't matter. I have a beautiful baby, and she is happy and healthy.

Brooke, age 26, mother of 1 daughter

My baby had colic and cried constantly when he was born. Somehow I survived!

Mary, age 29, mother of 1 infant son

Your day becomes fully scheduled...every day from the day your child is born until the day that child becomes an adult and moves out. It will be tough, but you won't mind it like you'd assume you would!

My trick is to think about every time I wake with my baby as just "one more time." It certainly won't be only one more time, but I think dealing with the exhaustion and struggle is like approaching a marathon with a mindset of "I just have to make it through the next mile." It doesn't make it less exhausting, but it helps break it up and seem more manageable. Just think about getting through the next 10 minutes, one hour, or one day. Deal with the rest as it comes.

Kelly, age 31, mother of 1 son

You have to have a lot of patience. Everything takes five times as long, from getting in the car to making breakfast, not to mention the dirty diapers and tantrums.

Greta, age 31, mother of 1 son

Staying connected to my spouse. Our life drastically changed when we had a baby.

One day, when our baby was 2 months old, and I was having trouble breastfeeding and she was constipated, I looked at my husband and said, "When was the last time we talked about anything but my boobs or her poop?"

Michelle, age 31, mother of 1 infant daughter

Balancing motherhood with working full-time. I'm constantly struggling with—is this the right thing to do?

I enjoy my job, but I feel guilty if I have to stay home because my son is sick and needs me, and I feel guilty if I go to work and I'm not home with him.

You get lots of advice from everywhere. With today's technology it's too easy to compare yourself with other moms and wonder if you are doing things right—it's actually stressful.

Erin, age 31, mother of 1 son

I don't have enough time for anything!

Linda, age 32, mother of 1 son & twin daughters

I wish I wasn't so hard on myself.

I wish I didn't worry about what other people think.

I struggled with breastfeeding. My son was tongue and lip-tied. I was pumping non-stop. Then I got an infection. I was miserable and felt so ashamed. I put so much pressure on myself. When I finally stopped, because I just couldn't do it anymore, a huge weight was lifted off my shoulders.

Andrea, age 32, mother of 1 son

I had several miscarriages. It was traumatic. I worried that I would never have a baby. So now, I'm grateful every day—even when my kids are naughty and I'm exhausted.

Juanita, age 33, mother of two sons

I am learning to put away my phone and laptop so I'm less distracted. Looking at facebook and reading emails isn't as important as being fully there with my kids.

Carly, age 34, mother of 3 daughters

My husband and I never have any time as a couple. Parenting never ends! I miss the fun we used to have together BC (before children).

Eleana, age 35, mother of 1 son & 1 daughter

Knowing that I am molding these kids into adults, and hoping that I'm not screwing them up too badly.

Katie, age 36, mother of 3 sons & 1 daughter

Being able to go through this process of being a single mother and feeling adequate to my kids. Letting things be the imperfect perfect for us that they are.

Mindy, age 36, mother of 2 children

Julie Gohman, Ph.D.

Saying NO. You just want to give them everything. I always feel guilty.

Trisha, Age 37, mother of 1 daughter & 1 son

When they get sick because I end up panicking. My worry is that I don't have the solution to the problem right away. Seeing them sick breaks my heart.

Consolata, age 37, mother of 2 daughters & 2 sons

Discipline! I'm fairly strict, and my husband is a big marshmallow, so we often disagree about how to handle things. It has been a source of tension and conflict between us.

Sasha, age 38, mother of 2 sons

My son has a lot of special needs. I cried and cried. I thought, what did I do to deserve this? Why me? I was mad at God. I felt ashamed and sorry for myself. Eventually I stopped asking why. We take it one day at a time. He is my son and I love him.

Maxie, age 39, mother of 1 son & 1 daughter

Mothering is like a flashlight on my most tender, vulnerable, and hidden joys and fears.

For me, some of the most challenging parts of mothering is getting hooked and triggered in my own perfection and pleasing tendencies when my daughter is struggling (especially when there's an audience).

It's easy for me to compare/despair, catastrophize, or worry that things will "always" be like this when there are crashing waves of anger, fear, or disrespect from my child. I've found the practice of mindfulness meditation extremely helpful to gain perspective, cultivate calm, and help me differentiate between my reactions and my child's.

Amy, age 39, mother of 1 daughter

Having to punish and "follow through" when my kids do wrong. We all make mistakes and none of us want to be judged or have it held against us, but with punishments come learning lessons.

Learning how to let go.

Desiree, age 40, mother of 2 sons & 1 daughter

Allowing my daughter to make her own mistakes. Letting her learn for herself about how to navigate friendships, boys, and school now that she's on her own.

Jessie, age 40, mother of 1 daughter

Keeping everything in perspective, like when I want a clean house, and I want to get places on time. I'm tempted to lose my cool. I have to stop and remember that ten years from now, I will forget the mess and the meeting, but the legacy I leave in the hearts of my children will last forever.

Kristi, age 40, mother of 2 sons & 1 daughter

Watching my children struggle, yet knowing by in my heart that when they overcome the struggle they will learn/grow.

Tina, age 40, mother of 1 daughter & 1 son

I wish they would listen more and understand that I do know a few things.

As much as they fight, I wish they knew that someday they are going to be good friends.

Angel, age 43, mother of 2 daughters & 1 son

Adjusting my parenting skills for each child - each child is unique and, therefore, need different things from me.

Jess, age 44, mother of 2 sons

The challenges of motherhood grow and change with each new developmental stage.

I used to think the lack of sleep was the most challenging when they were babies.

Then I thought the teen years were the most difficult...when their hearts were hurt and I couldn't fix it.

Now, the most challenging thing I face is being ready to send her off into the world....my heart isn't ready for that at all. I pray I gave her all the skills and wisdom needed to make good decisions and find happiness.

Amy, age 44, mother of 1 daughter & 1 son

Giving them enough freedom to make the mistakes they have to make. They're going to have to feel it for themselves. I ache for that, but I have to let them do it. It's my job to let them get messy, make mistakes, and learn to get back up.

Jenna, age 46, mother of 2 daughters

Feeling helpless when your child is in physical or emotional pain.

Bree, age 48, mother of 1 son & 1 daughter

Seeing them spread their wings and fly away. It's bittersweet.

Carla, age 49, mother of 2 sons

Discipline. I want them to have life lessons, but I want to guide them too.

There are so many things that you put off when you are a mother—I'm still waiting to make my bucket list.

Robin, age 49, mother of 3 daughters & 1 son

Grappling with, and adapting to, the ever present question of what do I have control of, what don't I have control of, and how I want to respond in my relationships with my children regarding these issues.

Lisa, age 50, mother of 4 daughters

Trying not to worry every time they go out the door. I throw out a little prayer every time.

I have found that over time, mothering becomes less physically demanding but becomes more emotionally demanding.

Theo, age 50, mother of 2 sons

Parenting adult children presents different challenges. Finding the correct balance between giving advice and being hands-off and letting them discover their own life.

Lucy, age 51, mother of 5 daughters

I find myself thinking about all the things I wished I had done differently when I was their age, and I try to talk to my kids, hoping they won't make the same mistakes that I did.

Jane, age 51, mother of 2 sons and 1 daughter

Sitting back and watching them make their own choices, and be the adults they now are.

To have enough time for all of them. Between work, my husband, and my own life, it's busy. I try to be fair to each one of them.

Jackie, age 52, mother of 2 daughters & 2 sons

Our children are a reflection of us as mothers, so it's hard when they misbehave-we feel the spotlight on us, and often think we somehow failed.

My job is to guide my children, to prepare them for this big beautiful world. It's a heavy responsibility that I take seriously.

I try to make good judgments, good decisions as a mother. It can be difficult to know how to handle every little curve ball that comes along.

I know I'll make mistakes, and I'm not perfect, but I give it my best every day.

When I see a mom at the grocery store with kids who are crying or misbehaving, I try to do something to help, or at the very least I say a little prayer. I remember how difficult it was to shop with little children.

I think a common challenge is not losing your relationship with your spouse. Not losing yourself.

When my children fight, I make them look at each other, apologize, forgive each other and hug each other. It usually ends in giggles and laughter.

Genny, age 53, mother of 4 daughters

The choice to work outside the home was not accepted when I was younger like it is now. I had to defend myself, mostly from other moms. I felt as though I wasn't a good mom because I worked. It caused me to question myself a lot. Thankfully I have a very supportive husband, who was an active parent, and we have a true partnership.

Kim, age 57, mother to 2 daughters & 1 son

Seeing my children's struggles and failures; allowing them to make mistakes with natural consequences and not jumping to step in and rescue them.

Chari, age 57, mother to 2 daughters & 1 son

The transition that I am experiencing these last few years, to being the mother of adult children, has been especially hard for me. I'm not exactly sure why. I know I am still loved, so it must be that I am not needed, so in part, my purpose is lost.

Jody, age 58, mother to 1 daughter & 1 son

When you have multiple children...making sure your kids feel they are equally loved and valued.

Annie, age 60, mother of 1 daughter & 3 sons

When any of my children are injured or hurt in some way, my heart breaks. I want to protect them, but I have to let go. They have to learn from their mistakes and stand on their own.

You have dreams for your children, but you end up realizing you just want them to be happy.

Ann, age 61, mother of 4 sons

Not trusting myself to follow my own instincts, to follow my own plans. To do things the way that I want to do them instead of doing what is expected, or what I think I am supposed to do.

Theresa, age 63, mother of 4 sons

You think when you have a child, you have them from birth to 18, but it's a continuous job; it's a lifetime commitment. You are always a parent.

I was a single parent, and tried to do everything for my son. I should have put my foot down more, and let him do more for himself. It's hard when you are trying to be both mother and father to a child.

Elaine, age 63, mother of 1 son

Discipline, setting limits, I'm not good at that. And keeping everything organized.

Sharon, age 65, mother of 1 daughter

The teenage years, as they get older, there is so much more going on.

Laurie, age 65, mother of 2 sons

I tend to take on my daughters feelings, whether it is joy, pain, happiness or sorrow.

I want to fix everything for them, and it's just not possible.

Sally, age 67, mother of 2 daughters

Letting go.

Finding a different purpose once they are grown.

Having my adult children live out-of-state and not having regular contact, not seeing them very often. I miss being involved in their lives.

Marilyn, age 68, mother of 3 daughters & 1 son

I was only 19 when I got married to my high school sweetheart, and 20 when I had my first child. I always knew I wanted children and I loved my babies, but I was very young, and probably missed out on things with my girlfriends.

My challenges as a mother were made easier because of all the support I had from both sets of grandparents, who lived close by.

Sandy, age 70, mother of 1 son & 1 daughter

Keeping my mouth shut.

I still want them to come home—but with both parents working, teenagers in everything, and some distance—it's hard. They must have their lives I realize, but they were my life for so long. Now I hear my parents saying, "please, please come home."

Mary, age 71, mother of 1 daughter & 2 sons

Julie Gohman, Ph.D.

Time. I always wish I had more time.

Shari, age 72, mother of 1 son & 1 daughter

How to be a good mother-in-law.

Finding that appropriate place where I can be part of the lives of my sons and their families where I feel useful, and even appreciated, but acknowledges that they are an independent family. What's my place?

How to communicate openly and honestly with my adult children and their spouses.

Judy, age 75, mother of 4 sons

Balancing bringing home the bacon and being a mother. I had a very demanding job that I loved, and I also loved being a mother.

My ex-husband was an alcoholic and so we divorced when our kids were in 2nd and 5th grade. I was on my own as a single mom for many years. I was both mom and dad to my children. The one thing I wanted my kids to learn was perseverance.

Jackie, age 82, mother of 2 daughters

If my boys fought, I told them to go out behind the barn.

My idea was to work'em hard and they won't get into mischief.

I never had the cops at my door and I never had any issues with drugs, though I can't say they didn't try'em.

Arlene, age 84, mother of 7 boys & 1 daughter

I was so busy all the time, from early in the morning to late at night. It was a lot of work keeping my children in clothes and well fed.

We lived by the river, so I had to watch them careful so they didn't go down the river or drown. Thankfully, none of them did.

Lu, age 91, mother of 5 daughters & 1 son

Trying to look on the good side, encouraging them, and being positive, even lighthearted, when your children are going through something difficult.

To be a good mother, I think it's important not to embarrass my children.

Nadine, age 93, mother of 2 daughters

When you are faced with challenges, remember the old saying, "this too shall pass."

In memory of Grandma Bobbie, age 95, mother of 6 daughters & 3 sons

If I could go back in time and give myself some words of wisdom, it would be...

Don't worry about what other people think. Just do your best.

Bella, age 21, mother of 1 infant son

Find an older woman who you trust, who is a good mother, and follow her example.

Sophie, age 24, mother of 1 infant daughter

Listen to your own instincts. DO what is right for you and your baby.

Kate, age 25, mother of 1 infant son

Keep calm. Don't stress. You'll get everything done eventually.

Abby, age 25, mother of 1 infant daughter

Parenting is a team effort. Help each other. Communicate. Be there.

Maria, age 29, mother of 1 daughter & 1 son

If you are exhausted, rest. If you feel like crying, cry. It's okay to be human.

Calinda, age 30, mother of twin boys

Open your heart, love, don't be afraid of getting hurt, and BREATHE!

Carrie, age 31, child care mother of many infants

Get a journal. Write more down. You think you'll never forget, but you do.

Erin, age 31, mother of 1 son

Every baby is going to develop at their own pace. It doesn't mean there's anything wrong with them. Take the baby books as a guideline not a bible.

Just because you screw up one day doesn't make you a bad mom.

Michelle, age 31, mother of 1 infant daughter

Much of parenting, and even childbirth, is beyond your control. Relax. Let go.

Go with the flow more, it will all work out.

Let your spouse and other people in your life care for your child in their own way. Know they are doing their best. Your child will still be alive when you get back.

Greta, age 31, mother of 1 son

Every child, and parent, does everything at their own pace. Other parents' advice comes from what worked best for them. In the end, you, your partner, and your baby will figure out what works for you (all of you) - and it may be something something totally different.

Don't hang on other people's realities or expectations when you have your own family to be responsible to.

Kelly, age 31, mother of 1 son

Don't be afraid to ask for help.

Linda, age 32, mother of 1 son and twin daughters

Be more confident and do what is best for you and your baby.

Don't worry about what other people think so much.

You have to learn on your own. You have to experience it for yourself.

Andrea, age 32, mother of 1 son

Let things go. They always work out in the end. Might not be what you thought but they open the door for better things.

Mindy, age 36, mother of 2

Don't take yourself too seriously. You will find some awesome friends. They will save you.

Katie, age 36, mother of 3 sons & 1 daughter

When they are little, you think it's going to last forever because it consumes so much of you—being up all night, changing dirty diapers—but it actually flies by. Listen when people say "don't blink" because before you know it they're all grown up.

Trisha, age 37, mother of 1 daughter & 1 son

Time spent wisely leads to bliss.

If you learn to take responsibility for your own life, motherhood will be like a play well rehearsed.

Consolata, age 37, mother of 2 daughters & 2 sons

Pay attention to resentment when it bubbles up - it's a powerful tool that can shine a light on what's out of alignment.

If I could go back in time and give myself some words of wisdom, it would be...

Offer peace, comfort, rest, compassion and grace to yourself first and then to others. I can't sustainably give to others what I can't offer and provide for myself.

Boundaries matter.

Self compassion trumps all.

Amy, age 39, mother of 1 daughter

Giving choices and options is important. You keep some control while letting them make some of their own decisions.

Recognize that so many things are minor. If you think about it, they are really insignificant in the big picture.

Not having control is not a bad thing.

You can have a plan, but you need to be able to adapt and be flexible when things go off schedule (as they always do).

Jessie, age 40, mother of 1 daughter

Set your boundaries - even with children.

Don't smother them or shelter them from the world. Teach them how to face the world, not run from it.

Lead by example! In time, they will respect you.

Desiree, age 40, mother of 2 sons & 1 daughter

The greatest GIFT we can give our children is to be fully PRESENT!

Kristi, age 40, mother of 2 sons & 1 daughter

Be kind, to yourself.

Tina, age 40, mother of 1 daughter & 1 son

You think they are going to be little forever, but it all goes by so fast. As the saying goes – the days are long but the years are short.

Angel, age 43, mother of 2 daughters & 1 son

Spend more quality time interacting with your children - not just watching them in their activities or doing homework together. Spend time getting to know their likes, dislikes, thoughts, ideas, dreams, etc.

Jess, age 44, mother of 2 sons

Relax. It's all going to be okay.

Savor the moments. Laugh a little more. Let loose a bit and don't try to over-manage things.

Amy, age 44, mother of 1 daughter & 1 son

Be generous with your love and affection, time and attention— that's what they will remember the most from their time with you.

Arie, age 45, mother of 2 daughters & 1 son

You can't be a fabulous mom without taking care of yourself. You have to nurture and love yourself. It has to be a conscious effort. It's so easy to give yourself away until you're empty and have nothing left to share. But what about you?

Jenna, age 46, mother of 2 daughters

Don't worry so much.

Take a deep breath, smile, and enjoy every moment you can with them.

Be honest with your children.

Bree, age 48, mother of 1 son & 1 daughter

Slow down!

Robin, age 49, mother of 3 daughters & 1 son

We all question ourselves as moms, but kids are resilient, so don't beat yourself up if you make a mistake. If your kids know they are loved, then they are going to be okay.

Find people, find a support network, find other women with kids the same age, so you can know that what you are going through is normal and you're not alone.

As your kids grow up, you have to trust that you've done your job; you can't control everything. It's about letting go, letting them make mistakes so they can learn to deal with hardship when the consequences are minimal.

Theo, age 50, mother of 2 sons

Just show up, do your best and know you are enough, you do enough, and that it will be enough.

Relax and quit trying so hard. It will all work out.

Go confidently in the direction that you feel called, asking the Holy Spirit to guide and protect you.

Lisa, age 50, mother of 4 daughters

Always say "I love you"—and be okay even if they don't say it back.

Cherish the hugs you get from your little boys. They grow up and become men, and you know they still love you, but you don't have the cuddling anymore.

Stop. Stand back. Take it all in. Be aware of what's happening during moments with your children, and put that in your memory.

Jane, age 51, mother of 2 sons and 1 daughter

I was young when I first became a mother, but by the time I had my youngest son I was older and more relaxed. I'm so much less uptight than I was at first about everything. So, I say...

Don't sweat the small stuff.

Enjoy all the little moments.

Let things go.

Jackie, age 52, mother of 2 daughters & 2 sons

As moms, we think we have to do it all. So much pressure. So much blame. But it's okay to take help. And to know we are not the only ones influencing our children.

Try to be more patient and gentle with your children when you are trying to teach them or correct their behaviors.

Take a deep breath when you're wondering if your house will ever be clean again, or if the tantrums will ever stop, or if you'll ever get a good night's sleep. This too shall pass.

Take care of yourself, remember that when you're happy, you're a better parent.

Genny, age 53, mother of 4 daughters

You can have a solid career and you can raise great kids. You can't do it without a supportive partner or some kind of support system, but you can do it.

You can't do it all, but if you prioritize, you can do what's important.

Hire a housekeeper so you can take that guilt about not having the perfectly clean house off your plate.

Kim, age 57, mother of 2 daughters & 1 son

Nothing is ever as idyllic as you imagine or want it to be; accept what it is without being disappointed. Making mistakes is a part of life, it will be ok!

Chari, age 57, mother of 2 daughters & 1 son

Do not beat yourself up over things you did, or didn't do.

You can only be yourself. You can't be anyone else.

Jody, age 58, mother of 1 daughter & 1 son

Treasure each day as you are taking care of them, working, feeding, teaching, cleaning, playing, praying, and singing. You are creating the basis for an incredible person that is your child.

Annie, age 60, mother of 1 daughter & 3 sons

Spend more time with your children—playing with them, listening to them.

It's okay to have unwashed laundry, dirty dishes. The most important thing is TIME with your children.

Tell your children you love them every single day.

Ann, age 61, mother of 4 sons

Trust yourself. Be kind to yourself.

Theresa, age 62, mother of 4 sons

You think when you give in to your children, you are making them happy, but actually you need to have some tough love at times to teach them responsibility.

Elaine, age 63, mother of 1 son

Hire a housekeeper.

Focus on your child.

Journal more about the everyday stuff so you have a keepsake to give your child.

Sharon, age 65, mother of 1 daughter

Find a partner who will share parenting duties, someone who has similar values and ideas about family. Talk about your expectations. Don't let yourself end up with all the work of raising the kids and taking care of the house by yourself.

Laurie, age 65, mother of 2 sons

Take better care of yourself along the way.

Make good women friends and strive to stay in touch through the years.

Marilyn, age 68, mother of 3 daughters & 1 son

Give yourself more patience. When the baby is crying or won't take a nap, or being fussy, it's so overwhelming. Let it go, be patient, realize in the grand scheme of things, it's not that big of a deal.

Sandy, age 70, mother of 1 son & 1 daughter

Hold them close. Keep giving those butterfly kisses.

Shari, age 72, mother of 1 son & 1 daughter

Take time for each child.

See each child as an individual.

Judy, age 75, mother of 4 sons

Your little ones think you're doing the right thing, so relax, don't keep second-guessing everything. You're not always going to get it right, but they don't know that.

It is not what happens in your life, but how you react to it. The right attitude and perseverance can do wonders.

Jackie, age 82, mother of 2 daughters

Always keep the lines of communication open with your kids.

Patience!

Arlene, age 84, mother of 7 sons & 1 daughter

Try to be patient and understanding with your children, even when they are naughty.

Lu, age 91, mother of 5 daughters & 1 son

Be more observant about what's happening in your children's lives so you are able to counsel them if they need help.

Try to be positive, instead of negative, when difficult things come up so that your children feel they can confide in you. Be encouraging and help them take the right path.

Nadine, age 93, mother of 2 daughters

Julie Gohman, Ph.D.

Love each one of your children unconditionally. All that love will come back to you.

There is no limit to how much you can love.

**In memory of Grandma Bobbie, age 95,
mother of 6 daughters & 3 sons**

Research Details

The women I interviewed for my research study were an exceptional, yet normal group of women. They included those who experienced unplanned teenage pregnancies, physical and emotional abuse, and poverty. Some had children with serious disabilities and/or disease. They included single parents who had a partner in the military, or in prison, or who died suddenly. Others functioned as single parents by choice. Some women went through intense crises about their identity, sexuality, body image, or ability to maintain a healthy partnership while parenting small children. Many were in the middle of major changes—recreating their lives after a divorce, beginning a new career, or letting go of grown children and moving on to the next stage of life.

The women in this study were normal in that they each had their own struggles, no different than any of us, yet they were exceptional because they were willing to open their hearts and share their stories about motherhood with me.

Their stories do not have neat beginnings and endings, rather, like most women, they continue on, day by day. They continue striving for balance in their lives, constantly readjusting as their children get older, as needs change, and as they come to know themselves better.

The women in this study included those who were married, divorced, remarried, widowed, and single. Number of children ranged from one child to eight children (including stepchildren). The stage of motherhood varied—some were busy with little children, others had teenagers, and a few had adult children. Several were also grandmothers.

Most of the women were heterosexual. I also interviewed one bisexual mother, and one lesbian mother.

Many different ethnicities were represented: Caucasian, South Asian, Latino, Native American, and African American. They lived in both rural and urban areas; and represented a wide spectrum in socio-economic class. Some women would be considered poor, some middle class, and some quite wealthy.

About half the women were Christian, a third were not religious in the traditional sense (several expressed being spiritual and/or interested in all religions), one woman was Wiccan, and another indicated her religion was an earth-based feminine spirituality and Unitarian.

The women ranged in their educational level from having completed their GED, to technical training, to a 4-year college degree, to completing graduate school. Most were college educated.

Two-thirds of the women worked full-time. One woman worked part-time. One woman was a homemaker. Another woman was a graduate student. One woman was re-establishing her career. The oldest woman that I interviewed was retired.

I have deliberately omitted (or changed, with permission) some information about the women I interviewed that was not critical to their narrative for this book, such as: names, ethnicity, religious affiliation, age, education, location, career, socio-economic status, and other private information (with exceptions where appropriate). The focus in this book is on their experiences of motherhood.

My complete research study is available through academic library portals, listed under my name: Julie Gohman, Sofia University, 2014, with the title: "A Narrative Inquiry Exploring the Experiences of Women Who Embrace Motherhood." However, I suspect not everyone wants to read a 300-page academic paper, which is what you will find if you look up my research. Of course, I think it's great reading and don't hesitate to recommend it.

The final three chapters are quotes from real women who I know personally as family and friends, or from women I have met at various events and places as I was writing this book. These chapters were not part of my academic research, but something I added for fun.

Thank you to all the women who were willing to open up and share their experiences of motherhood with me. Your stories and quotes are a beautiful gift to all of us. Blessings to you.

In love and light,
Julie

About Julie

J ulie Gohman, Ph.D., received her doctorate in Psychology from Sofia University in Palo Alto, CA and is a member of the Society for Humanistic Psychology and the Association for Transpersonal Psychology. She also earned degrees in Human Development and Education.

She lives in Minnesota with her family, which includes her husband, two teenage sons, two dogs, two cats, and a parakeet named Skippy.

She is the author of *10 Sacred Questions for Every Woman About Love, Friendship and Finding True Happiness.* Her next book, *The Secret Life of a Mother: How Motherhood Changes You Forever* will be coming out soon.

To learn more please visit juliegohman.com

Made in the USA
Charleston, SC
16 May 2016